MOVING MOUNTAINS

MOVING MOUNTAINS

Coping with Change in Mountain Communities

SARA NEUSTADTL

Appalachian Mountain Club
BOSTON, MASSACHUSETTS

MOVING MOUNTAINS
Coping with Change in Mountain Communities
by Sara Neustadtl

Editorial direction: Aubrey Botsford
Production: Renée M. Le Verrier
Cover design and illustration: Bonnie Dann

ISBN: 0-910146-63-2

5 4 3 2 1 86 87 88 89

For Frank P. Davidson

Acknowledgements

I owe a very large debt of thanks to the imagination and guidance of Frank P. Davidson, of the Massachusetts Institute of Technology (MIT), and to Arlyn Powell, formerly the publisher at the Appalachian Mountain Club. I am grateful as well to Professor Jack Ives of the University of Colorado in Boulder, whose extensive experience, knowledge, and storytelling ability lent this project both shape and direction. He is president of the International Mountain Society and editor of the *Journal of Mountain Research and Development,* which continues to be the primary source of information on mountain environments throughout the world.

My thanks are also due to Professor K.S. Valdiya in Nainital, India. Both he and his colleagues in the Central Himalayan Environment Association made an invaluable link to information and activity in that region.

I thank all the people mentioned within these pages, and take the opportunity here to thank others who also have been generous with their gifts of time and thoughtfulness. I will not forget Sue Cottingham and Sheila Murray in Crested Butte for their informative discussions and hospitality. Thanks to Professor Gernot Patzelt, who made available the many resources of the

University of Innsbruck and the Alpine Research Station in Obergurgl. In northern California, Tim McKay, Chris Jennican, Joe Gillespie, Tom Parsons, and the Northcoast Environmental Center in Arcata all generously opened doors and files to me. I am obliged to Kavita Ram Shresta in Nepal, whose expertise and boundless good humor are very much appreciated. I extend thanks, as well, to Gabriel Campbell at the Community Forestry Development Project, to the courteous and helpful people at the Nepal Australia Forestry Project and the Swiss Association for Technical Assistance, and to Dr. Ratna S.J.B. Rana for his help and that of the Nepal National Planning Commission.

Here in Boston, I continue to value Carol Verburg's long-term support and wise editorial advice. Lastly, my deepest thanks go to Peter Molnar for his contributions both at home and in the mountains.

CONTENTS

Foreword

by Arlene Blum

WHEN most of us think of mountains, the images we have are of peace and beauty. We go to the hills to share their serene beauty. But for people living among them, mountains can prove a harsh and difficult environment in which to survive. Traditionally, mountain people have always faced problems of natural origin: poor soil, extremes of rainfall and climate, steep rocky terrain, difficult trails. Now the mountain areas are becoming increasingly valued by many city dwellers, and the man-made pressures of population, tourism, and development are coming to the most remote regions.

Stories of impending environmental disasters regularly make headlines. We are saddened to hear that the Himalaya are washing into the Bay of Bengal; that mines, logging, and tourists threaten our fragile wilderness areas. The problems seem so large and complex that most of us can only sigh at the loss and turn to our own affairs.

Fortunately, Sara Neustadtl decided to do more. She began to investigate how mountain peoples around the world were facing these diverse obstacles. And, based on her extensive research, she shares with us a series of fascinating accounts about how mountain dwellers are dealing with a variety of threats to their way of life and livelihood. These inside stories are as gripping and readable as good fiction and so much more poignant for being true.

Included are such diverse accounts as how Crested Butte, Colorado, warded off a billion-dollar molybdenum mine; how Obergurgl, in the Austrian Alps, voluntarily limited marriages, and later hotels, in order to prevent overcrowding; how a Nepalese farmer managed to set up a successful reforestation project; and how several elderly Yurok Indians in northern California prevented the U.S. Forest Service from building a logging road through their sacred mountains.

The inherent drama in these tales is amplified by the author's curiosity about the lives of village people. These are not the typical journalistic stories of impending disaster, but sensitive personal accounts of remarkable people and their reactions to change in their way of life.

* * * * *

My own mountain experience has been primarily climbing in North America, the Himalaya, the Andes, and Africa. As a climber, I focused my attentions on the uninhabited rock and ice summits. But on my way to climb high peaks, such as Everest and Annapurna, I came to appreciate more and more the amazingly beautiful little villages where I suspected the really interesting dramas were taking place. I always wanted to understand more about the villagers: what the women exuberantly call to each other as they weed the fields and gather wood; what the men are chuckling about over cards in the tea shop; the children's games. I wanted to know what is important to these people who live in the shadow of the world's highest and most stunning mountains.

So I planned a 10-month, 2,000-mile trek the length of the

Himalayan range, from Bhutan to Ladakh. I studied the Nepali language and, along the way enjoyed many basic conversations in Nepalese. Our talks usually focused on where and why we are traveling, our families, and our fields and farm animals. Extreme sympathy is usually expressed at my lack of children, and disbelief that people so rich as we trekkers obviously are have no cows, no pigs, no water buffalo, not even a single chicken. Family, fields, and animals are major subjects of conversation in a language where there are four different words for uncle or aunt and at least sixteen for cousin.

And seeing us strolling along, perpetually on vacation, with gear costing more than the average Nepalese hill family would earn in five years, some villagers begin to question their way of life, saying: "We are so poor. You are so rich. I want to go back to America with you."

But I find that reassuring them is not too difficult: "In America, people work all the time to make money. They must live in big crowded cities and always hurry. Here in Nepal, you have less money, but you have peace, religion, your family, your fields, and your animals."

And indeed increasing numbers of Westerners are spending thousands of dollars and traveling thousands of miles to share the harmonious life of the Nepalese hill farmer. They return home cherishing memories of the deep-blue high-altitude sky framing the icy peaks; a lammergeyer soaring through the high crisp air; the emerald-green terraced fields dotted with villages whose natural architecture is so much more in harmony with the landscape than our carefully planned developments.

For many visitors, the high point of their long and expensive journey is a few hours in a humble farmer's home drinking sweet cardamon tea and exchanging conversation via a child who speaks some English. But for those of us who cannot physically journey to the Himalaya, reading *Moving Mountains* is like spending time in a cosy kitchen in one of those beautiful little villages, learning what mountain people think and want and what is important to them.

I cannot help but marvel at how Sara Neustadtl gained all this detailed and personal information. Was she a mouse at a Himalayan hearth, a listening owl in a Rocky Mountain forest? However she learned it all, we must be grateful to her for sharing with us these fascinating stories and for presenting them to us in such a readable and interesting fashion.

* * * * *

There is a brief story told by Hebrew mystics of the poor Rabbi Eisek who lived in the ghetto of Cracow. The pious Rabbi had a recurrent dream enjoining him to jouney to distant Prague where he would find a hidden treasure to end his poverty. After much difficult travel he reached Prague, where he could not find any treasure. Instead, his journey was rewarded by the information that the treasure was buried beneath the stove in his own home back in Cracow. Hurrying home, the Rabbi dug in a neglected portion of his house and indeed found a treasure that put an end to all his misery.

And so we too must sometimes journey to exotic and faraway places to learn what is in our own hearts and homes. In our communities we meet with obstacles as profound and difficult as those faced by the mountain people in this book. In reading these accounts of their courageous and imaginative solutions, we should all obtain inspiration about how we can solve problems in our own lives.

Introduction

ETERNITY isn't what it used to be. Time was when mountains were gods and, like the gods, eternal.

Who wouldn't assume that mountains have been there, unchanged, since the beginning of time? Seldom was permanence so manifest, so easily turned into myth. From Olympus, Zeus lobbed thunderbolts. Prometheus was chained to the Caucasus. Popocatapetl was the entrance to hell, Agoeng the navel of the world. Chomolungma was the goddess mother of the world and Kailash the throne of Shiva. Haraberagaiti fastened heaven to the center of the world. Gods infested Fuji, Khumbila, Shasta, Denali, Katahdin; Tacoma actually was god. All were peaks where earth met the divine.

In Hebrew legend, God tossed lumps of dirt over the water to make land, and the pebbles inside the clods exploded to become mountains. Another Hebrew legend has mountains darting about like birds until the deity captured them and fastened them down. Hopi myth has it that Poqanghoya squeezed the higher places on earth in order to solidify them, while he kindly left the lower places soft enough to hoe.

Christian tradition, too, has its share of mountain stories. In the Bible, mountains breached the ocean to give Adam and Eve a place to stand on the third day of Creation. According to the seventeenth-century English theologian Thomas Burnet, God punished Adam and Eve's original sin by triggering a kind of cosmic meltdown: the sun heated the world so intensely that it cracked like an egg, releasing water that had been waiting underground since the land sliced through the ocean on the third day. The leftover shards are now the mountains, wrote Burnet. His *Sacred Theory of the Earth* appeared in the same decade as Isaac Newton's ideas about gravity and motion.

Earlier in that century another thinker had pondered the creation of mountains. Descartes explained that the earth had congealed from a spinning vortex thrown from the sun. He postulated that mountains formed when the spinning, cooling blob at the heart of the vortex shrank and wrinkled up like a dried apple. According to Descartes, who still looked toward a connection with a single act of creation, it was a divine pitch that had spun the vortex into motion.

Some Europeans broke from the traditional belief that mountains had existed since Genesis. Leonardo da Vinci, with his artist's eye for the particular, was among those who noticed the conundrum presented when he discovered shells on the tops of mountains. In his notebooks, he described his discoveries in the Apennines: "These shells remained walled up and dead beneath this mud, which became raised to such a height that the bed of the sea emerged into the air. And now these beds are of so great a height that they have become hills or lofty mountains." His logic was unusual for the time; unfortunately, he kept his thoughts locked up in private notebooks that were to remain unpublished during his lifetime.

The Chinese never bothered to look back toward an initial act of creation. Instead they put faith in the idea, imported from India by Buddhist priests, of a world that is periodically destroyed, remade, and destroyed again. Shells on a Chinese mountaintop are a confirmation, not a riddle. In *Science and Civilization in China,* Joseph Needham quotes the twelfth-century neo-Confucian philosopher Chu Hsi: "I have seen on high mountains conchs and oyster shells, often embedded in the rocks. These rocks in ancient times were earth or mud, and the conchs lived in water. Subsequently, everything that was at the bottom came to be at the top, and what was originally soft became solid and hard. One should meditate deeply on such matters, for these facts can be verified."

According to Needham, the Chinese term for geological time is originally a Taoist word indicating land that had either been covered by sea or would be at some time in the future. So commonplace was this assumption of eternal inversion that the third-century leader Tu Yu had his accomplishments inscribed on rocks in duplicate, setting one at the bottom of a mountain and burying the other at the top, in the belief that the rocks would change places over time.

* * * * *

Classical Chinese thinkers believed not in the eternity of mountains, then, but in the timelessness of change. To my surprise my research has led me to a similar conclusion.

In October 1976, Claire Sterling published an article in *The Atlantic Monthly* reporting that huge islands had begun to form in the Bay of Bengal, at the mouth of the Ganges. She pointed out that the source of the Ganges was in the Himalaya, and that the watersheds there were experiencing the most severe erosion of their 50-million-year history. I later looked into the matter, and this is what I found.

Over the millennia, the Ganges has taken water and soil deposited in the rivers of the Himalaya and fashioned a good piece of what is now Bangladesh. As the river moves over its own detritus, its momentum decreases. Ever-finer particles drop out of the flow and filter down to the river bed. By the time the Ganges meets the sea it is moving so slowly that large amounts of fine sediment drift to the bottom, making a slight barrier that the river must circumvent. The Ganges has done this so many times that today it flows into the Bay of Bengal from over a dozen mouths. From these mouths come the remaining sediments, particles that have built the border islands of the Ganges delta, the Sundarbans.

One of the delta rivers, the Hariya Bhanga, marks the uneasy border between India and Bangladesh. The Hariya Bhanga is now laying out another island, first discovered by a cruising Indian Navy frigate in 1971. It soon appeared on British Admiralty charts as New Moore Island, and by 1974 was big enough to appear on satellite photographs. Within a decade of its emergence, the island measured more than 150 square miles and was still growing.

India and Bangladesh have both claimed it. India calls it Purbasha, "Hope of the East." Bangladesh expects less of the island and has named it South Talapatty. Frigates and gunboats from both sides hover threateningly, while satellite pictures have begun to spot another island-in-the-making in the bay.

According to a tongue-in-cheek editorial in *Rising Nepal,* Kathmandu's English-language newspaper, the new islands should probably be deeded to Nepal, since it was probably Himalayan, Nepali soil—stripped off the mountainsides in the country's ever-intensifying cycle of erosion—that was building them.

* * * * *

The pressures of subsistence farming in the thickly populated Himalaya have stripped the hills of their trees. There are no fuel alternatives. The hills hold few roads that could bring in fuel or fertilizer, and the people have little cash to buy them anyway, so they cut the wood for firewood and keep millions of animals to fertilize their fields with dung. Because people and animals must be fed, the land has been stripped of trees: for firewood, for fodder, and in order to build terraced farms. The hills are left with little protection from the heavy rains of the monsoon season, and the soil washes away, leaving infertile subsoil on the hills and clogging the rivers with dirt.

The destruction of the mountains' soil base leads to a flood-drought cycle that is passed all the way down the river to the sea. Floods are only half the problem: as mountain soil compacts, hillside springs dry up, and the winter flow of the rivers decreases. Today, in the dry season, the Ganges carries barely enough water for all its users.

Not only in the Himalaya are mountains changing. Once-remote mountains all over the world are everywhere overrun by a modern rush for resources. In the last twenty-five years, nearly every mountain range in the world has been invaded—by miners, tourists, farmers, foresters. Even biting mountain air can become stale from the crowds who now come to breathe it. Both the Alps and the Rockies have been transformed into playgrounds for skiers, second-home buyers, and tourists. The Alps now support nine million people, while twenty-two million more regularly use them for entertainment. The homes, roads, and businesses that have sprung up to serve them all are causing an urban-style blight that is destroying the very beauty the visitors come to seek.

Mountains are now netted in freeways that deliver them to the plains. Inaccessible mountain brushwood is upgraded to timber status, sawed down, and hauled away. Overcrowding in the valleys shoves farmers to the higher ground, as people homestead slopes that once saw only the disappearing heels of nomads. In Colorado, mining engineers are exploring the unprecedented problem of how to dispose of an entire, pulverized mountain.

* * * * *

I was born and raised in the Midwest, and until I was twenty I never saw anything taller than September corn or an oak tree. I believe I did see some high hills when I was nineteen and passing through Tennessee one night on the way to Florida, but all those twinkling lights on the horizon could have been stars. The next year, in a Volkswagen van with several disreputable friends, I rode to the West Coast. We drove straight through. The first sunup came somewhere in Nebraska, which I found much like Illinois—more wheat, less corn. The second sunrise came just over the border in Utah, as the road passed through a snug mountain-ringed valley—ranch house below, cattle on the range, snowpack above. It was the first time in my life I had experienced anything other than sky over my head. Not many people can appreciate the shock I felt. I think I am fascinated by mountains to this day because I still can't believe that solid ground can exist so high up.

I didn't like the idea that all this high ground was disappearing. When faced with a problem, especially when one is living in a university community as I was a few years ago, one studies it. I was on the staff of an MIT magazine, *Technology Review*, and had the luck to be befriended by a man who is extraordinary even by MIT's standards. Frank Davidson is the inventor of the field of macro-engineering; a thirty-year backer of the English Channel tunnel; the originator of such concepts as artificial islands, a transnational supersonic subway, the national bicycling-jogging-hiking-bridle trail system, the trans-Sahelian aqueduct, and a citizen concerned with mountains.

At a meeting in Munich in 1974, Frank had tried to help the Germans and the United Nations formulate a plan of attack in order to save the Himalaya from deforestation, erosion, and overuse. This had led to the creation of the International Mountain Society and its attendant journal. To my knowledge this remains the only international forum for scientists involved with applying their work to problems in the mountains. The Munich group proposed, among other studies, surveys of erosion rates, and its members made a commitment to the formation of the International Center for Integrated Mountain Development, which was founded in 1983 with headquarters in Kathmandu.

Frank, a very democratically oriented thinker, thought someone ought to write a book, so that everyone could learn about the threat to the mountains. This is it.

* * * * *

It seemed quite reasonable to think that Nepal's problems with land overuse, deforestation, and erosion were but a small tip of a larger iceberg, and that if someone looked closely she would be able to discover parallel crises in mountain ranges the world over. It also seemed quite reasonable to assume that scientists had thought of the same thing, had studied the issue, and had found little essential links in some invisible ecological chain that was in danger of being severed. It stunned me to think of these wonderful landforms as fragile, their eternal mystery in danger of being snuffed out by accident.

Armed with my extensive experience in the field (a one-month commercial trek in Nepal) and my proof that the Himalaya was indeed melting away (Landsat pictures of the Bay of Bengal), I set off to write a book about the danger to the mountains and, more important, about what could be done to save them.

At Frank's suggestion, I looked in the dictionary for a word to encompass my new enthusiasm. There was "orography," the branch of geography that deals with mountains, but I wanted an "-ology," a "study of," rather than an "-ography," or "mapping of." Frank Davidson came up with a new word: "montology." Since that enthusiastic afternoon, the word has never been used. Montologists don't think of themselves as such. Their fields sit securely on branches of other trees: glaciology, meteorology, chemistry, geography, botany, physiology, hydrology, pedology, geology, anthropology, agronomy, forestry, ecology, archaeology, sociology—to name a few. There is not just a field here; there is an entire graduate school. I wanted to skim the cream off all these "-ologies" and use the resulting mix to show people how to fix what was going wrong in the mountains.

At the time, of course, I thought of mountains as a homogenous entity, like oceans or islands. I thought I could see clearly all the things mountains have in common. For example, all mountains seem to function within a separate biotic reality. They are precarious platforms for life. There is the omnipresent slope. Soil collects in the dips and is swept away from the outcrops. There is climatic discipline. Mountains' many life forms are arranged on the vertical: the southern flank of the Himalaya has tropical bamboo in its valleys and snow at its peaks, only a few miles away. The range of adaptation is a tribute to mountains' extremes and to life's tenacity.

Within the mountains, valleys barely a shout apart support people of different languages. On the scale of crawling lives, a dip serves the same divisive purpose as a chasm. Within severely imposed limits, all mountain inhabitants respond to life with procreation and growth, but the price of specialization is vulnerability to change. This holds for microbes, plants, animals, and humans.

High altitudes have more harsh ultraviolet radiation and amass less oxygen. Mountain climates fluctuate savagely, seasonally and diurnally. A perturbation that might be no more than a glitsch in the lowlands can cause death on a mountainside. After the 1815 eruption of the Tamburo volcano in Indonesia, most of Europe had some cool summers, but villages in the upper Alps stayed buried beneath the snow for two years. Slopes and climate limit growth. Soils build slowly. A misused mountainside may never recover. The second most-climbed mountain in the world is New Hampshire's Mount Monadnock—hikers have completely demolished the tender alpine vegetation that once grew on its rocky top.

The tread of hiking boots can cancel a colony of lichen in a single step. The sounds of machines can give bighorn sheep ulcers. People dynamite the heart out of a mountain and are puzzled when it caves in. The mark of our progress through the mountains is change. The flux is constant, but not steady, and often so very slow that we can look at a mountain and see no change, only eternity. So when the product of our labors makes itself known we are shocked and penitent, belatedly terrified by the seeming irreversibility of the changes that have been made.

* * * * *

These were the thoughts that prompted this book. I believed mountains were in great danger, and I thought science held the key to their survival. Both ideas turned out to be wrong.

To take the second idea first: it is indeed true that scientists are making responsible and conscientious efforts to apply their knowledge to solving the problems of people in the mountains, yet the scientists I talked to admit that they and the planners they advise are essentially helpless. Scientists can recommend more of many things: legislation, research, education, and investment in new and existing programs devoted to easing the life of mountain peoples and reversing the destruction of their environments. But we lowlanders have been bailing with these same buckets for years, and we know how slow the process is. As hard as I searched, I could find no generalized scientific prescription for mountains: their ills are too individual, having in each area as much to do with the mountains' physical characteristics as with a unique mélange of climate, land use, and human culture, tradition, and whim.

As for my other misconception: I have come to learn that the Himalaya is rising up as quickly, perhaps even more quickly, than it is being washed away. I have become more relaxed on the matter. But in the meantime I have met the mountain people. If even just the top few inches of the mountains wash away, what will happen to them?

The message of *Moving Mountains,* then, if there is one, is that mountain people are one endangered species with the power to prevent its own annihilation. Much to my surprise, a project that started off as a treatise on mountain ecology instead became a collection of stories about mountain people who have averted disaster in their mountain homes. Like the scientists, I have found no general prescription for success. (In fact, failure seemed a foregone conclusion in a few cases: I still don't know how some of my subjects pulled it off.) However, I do offer this talisman against discouragement: despite their minority status, their spiritual distance from the centers of wealth and power, and their physical isolation, the people I write about have saved themselves. They are the resident caretakers of massive hunks of the world's patrimony. It seems theirs are good hands.

* * * * *

Moving Mountains opens in a Rocky Mountain wilderness, an area with no resident human constituency. It does, however, have advocates. The Rocky Mountain Biological Laboratory (RMBL), in the Elk Mountains of the Rockies, houses scientists who hope that their work will inform decisions made in less pristine ranges. After sixty years, RMBL scientists are certain of two things: that they thoroughly understand neither the individual plants and animals in the mountain ecosystem nor the relationships among them. Though their haste is measured, these scientists are working against the clock. Their untouched natural laboratory, the wilderness, is disappearing. Even at RMBL there is acid rain, poisonous mine drainage in the streams, and the ever-present possibility of massive mineral finds. They're inspecting some of the tiniest rivets in the machinery of mountain life, and every discovery tells them how much more they have to learn.

In Crested Butte, down the valley from RMBL, people take a

more partisan view of science. There, a tribe of urban exiles staked its future on the belief that environmental research could expose the dangers of mining. Crested Butte was nearly a ghost town before the 1960s, when a few hundred hippie immigrants moved in. It wasn't long before their mountain refuge was invaded by American Metals Climax, Inc., (AMAX), a multibillion-dollar mining and mineral processing company bent on extracting a stupendous deposit of molybdenum from Crested Butte's nearest mountain—and taking the mountain along with it. With a corporate giant about to engulf their mountain hideaway, the newcomers mobilized to fight a quixotic battle. AMAX engineers knew they could design an environmentally sound mine, but they had to decide whether the company could afford to meet the exacting standards that the laws, backed by the people of Crested Butte, demanded.

Unlike the city-bred rebels of Crested Butte, the natives of Obergurgl, the highest parish in Austria's Tyrol, have behind them a millennium of mountain hardship. In the 1950s, the new skiing industry suddenly changed their age-old burden of winter snow into a bonanza. Within fifteen years the Gurglers had retooled their valley and built so many hotels that only postcards remained to remind them of what they had lost. A botany professor from a nearby village took it upon himself to rescue the villagers from their hell-bent expansion. At his request an international group of scientists combed the slopes for clues to the question, Where is the limit to Obergurgl's growth? The Gurglers learned that, despite today's technology, mountains make their own demands.

One hundred years ago the Gurglers were plagued by the limits of their environment: too many people to feed, not enough trees for firewood, not enough usable land. The Himalaya today is in danger from the erosion, flooding, and landslides that accompany these same pressures. European mountaineers saved themselves by finding alternative sources of energy and income, and they're helping Nepal's mountain people find ways to do the same. In Nepal, the Swiss build cheeseries. In some parts of the country, this has been a successful cultural graft; in Jugepani Pauwa, a village in the southernmost mountains, the graft didn't take. There, Swiss technicians planned an experimental appropriate-technology showpiece. Water, wood, and kerosene are all appallingly hard to come by in Pauwa, so the cheesery there was designed to use solar panels to warm biogas digesters. Gas from the digesters would heat vats of milk. Whey, a by-product of cheesemaking, would feed the pigs that produced the dung that filled the biogas digesters. Where the idea failed, and why, has as much to do with cultural misunderstandings and individual personalities as with imperfect technologies.

The central cause of deforestation in Nepal is the depredations wrought by people and animals gleaning fuel and food. Caught in a cycle of poverty and daily need, the people are destroying their own mountains. The diagnosis is the same throughout the Himalaya. The cure? Laxman Dong Tamung, a most unusual headman, solved the deforestation problem in his own district not with science or rational argument, nor even with the help of foreign development experts, but instead with a new twist on an old philosophy: thou shalt not kill, even if it's only a tree.

In other places, the flow between modern science and technology on the one hand and traditional mountain wisdom on the other reverses direction. Between the Himalaya and the Karakorum lies Ladakh, "Little Tibet," a harsh mountain desert on the border between India and China. The Ladakhis' culture harmonizes with their taxing and impoverished environment. To deal with privation they practice a religion that renounces not merely possessions but even their desire for them. The society embodies the Ghandian village ideal, or so it seemed to Helena Norberg Hodge, an Englishwoman who arrived in Ladakh the first year it was opened to foreign tourists. She feared that

Ladakh's rich heritage would be destroyed by imported Western values and the technologies that support them. Now, while the Indian government builds hydroelectric dams and factories and the tourists tempt the people with cameras and down jackets, Hodge imports simple techniques for home heating. The Ladakhis themselves are serene in the face of change. They welcome any technology, mainstream or alternative, that doesn't deflect them from their real goal: the traditional pursuit of enlightenment.

Like the Ladakhis, the Yurok and Karuk Indians of California's Siskiyou Mountains have charged their mountains with spiritual significance. To the U.S. Forest Service, the mountains have a more quantifiable value. The USFS can produce ample documentation to back its claim that the mountains can be roaded and logged without irreparable harm, but the Yuroks and Karuks don't accept this notion. To these Native Americans the mountains are sacred, the only remaining connection they have with the great spirit of the world. In anguished protests to the USFS they sought to explain that a people cut off from its god is no longer a people, but because they seek god on a mountain they are vulnerable. Their fate is arbitrated by law, and human law is not an accurate yardstick for the undefined.

* * * * *

Now that most of the world's mountains have been explored, the challenge is not to win them but to know them. Science and technology can fill that need, and they are increasingly important as the rate of change in the mountains quickens. For people who "think like a mountain," though, as Aldo Leopold advised, mountains are less something to preserve than facts of life, like birth and death, hunger and joy. As such, they are not amenable to treatment by global prescription.

Once people take over a mountain, the mountain is no longer

the only thing on the horizon. This book is therefore not just about mountains but also about the symbiosis between individuals in human communities and their mountain environments. In order to survive, mountain peoples have already navigated among extremes of weather, slope, isolation, and privation. What they have learned guides their steps as they face change.

In *Losing Ground*, the landmark book about the worldwide curse of erosion and its attendant tragedies, Erik Ekholm ended a section about erosion in the mountains as follows:

> "It is generally easy to recommend technological answers to ecological problems. Political and cultural factors are invariably the real bottlenecks holding up progress. Changing the relationship of people to land in the mountains, as anywhere else, involves sensitive changes in the relationship of people to one another."

This is where *Moving Mountains* begins.

CHAPTER ONE

A Bowl of Mountain

NOT far west of the Great Divide, in the ghost town of Gothic, Colorado, there lives a group of people who make it their business to know how mountains work when things are not disturbed. Gothic is the home of the Rocky Mountain Biological Laboratory, or RMBL (the acronym is pronounced "rumble" by the locals), an independent, nonprofit research institute devoted to the study of the biology of mountain environments.

The road to Gothic runs northward out of the Gunnison Basin past the old Crested Butte cemetery, and continues upward for two miles. It follows the contours of the hills through yellow-flowered summer pastures and cuts through an enclave of empty condominiums in the ski town of Mount Crested Butte. To the right is the humped back of Crested Butte Mountain, where ski trails have been shaved through the forest.

For four miles beyond the ski town the dirt road rises and follows the side of a ridge, high above the East River. The river below teases its oxbowed way through a velveteen meadow. The road plunges through groves of aspen. Above the river the way is lined with barren hills red with mineralization. Quaking aspen grove, flowering meadow, the river below and the mountains above: the wilderness is graceful here. The road skids down to the river and flattens at the Gothic townsite.

Gothic hasn't been a real town for a hundred years. It was a booming silver camp in the 1880s, one of the many mountain mining towns that depended on Crested Butte for supplies. A hard-working miner discovered silver there one fall, the story goes, and before retreating from the high country for the winter he mentioned his luck to two trusted friends. When he returned in the spring, hundreds of miners greeted him from his secret spot, his two good friends among them. Later, after Ulysses S. Grant had finished his term as president and was touring Colorado, he asked to be shown the wildest mining camp in the territory. They took him to Gothic.

Gothic Mountain (12,625 ft.), which towers half a mile over it to the west, gave the town its name. The mountain got its name because of the symmetrical corrugations on its sheer face, which reminded early explorers of Gothic arches. A few remnants of the majestic glaciers that carved the corrugations remain, small patches of snow on the landscape. The road to Gothic runs northward out of the Gunnison Basin, past the old Crested Butte cemetery, and continues upward for two miles. It follows the contours of the hills through yellow-flowered summer pastures and cuts through an enclave of empty condominiums in the ski town of Mount Crested Butte. Just beyond the condominiums the asphalt stops. To the right is the humped back of Crested Butte Mountain, where ski trails have been slashed through the forest. From here on, travelers on the road can leave behind the commercialism of Mount Crested Butte: they are in the mountains.

Biologists have gathered here every summer since 1928, the year John C. Johnson, professor of biology at the state college in Gunnison, bought the seventy-acre site by paying off $200 in back taxes. Along with the land he also got the lawyer's cabin, the livery stable, and the town hall, all of which are still used, and for an extra $3 he got the Gothic Grand Hotel. Johnson negotiated the deal with the then-mayor and only resident of Gothic, Garwood Judd, who was so enthusiastic about Johnson's plans that he sold him some lots he didn't exactly own.

RMBL's reputation is based on its long-term studies of natural life in an undisturbed state. It has the oldest, most complete set of baseline data that exists on the biota of the Rockies. One researcher has been coming here for almost fifty years and her curiosity has yet to be satisfied. To duplicate the research that has been done at RMBL, the scientists would have to start all over again and spend fifty years somewhere else—if they could find a similar undisturbed area. Unfortunately, with the development boom that has hit the area, the biologists' habitat is as endangered as that of the plants and animals they study.

* * * * *

The Gunnison Basin is like a huge bowl in the Rockies that catches and momentarily holds everything that spills out of the mountains: plants, animals, air, and water. These mountains breathe, slowly inhaling and exhaling, once every twenty-four hours. By day the heated air in the valleys rises with a soft upslope breeze. By night the cold mountain air slips downward and collects in chill atmospheric pools in the valleys. Up on Gothic Mountain the winter temperature seldom goes below – 32 degrees F; 2,100 feet below in the town of Gunnison, where all the air from a ring of ranges tends to collect, temperatures of – 70 degrees F have been recorded.

Water is a critical commodity in this area. Most of the rim of the Gunnison Basin is part of the Continental Divide. Not fifty miles south of Gunnison, the water that slides downhill is caught by the Colorado; just fifty miles east, it slides into the Arkansas. Wherever it goes, all the water in these landlocked mountains has a long trip ahead of it. Along the way it will be used and reused, caught in reservoirs and diverted into irrigation ditches, run through hydroelectric turbines, and channelled through city mains. And all along the riverine highways, water is dissolving minerals.

Mountain communities that catch their water from surface runoff are particularly aware of those minerals. Coal Creek, which supplies Crested Butte's small reservoir, dallies for a while in beaver ponds; the marshland acts as a natural filter for the water and assures a pure supply. But just below the city pipe is a mine. Heavily mineralized underground water can use an old mine shaft as an easy channel to the surface. In many places the streams around old mines have literally been lined with minerals streaming from the shafts. Abandoned mines in the area are still a major source of the chemical and mineral wastes that find their way into the West's water, and new mining is an actual or potential threat on many of the Gunnison Basin's headwater streams. The old Silver Spruce mine, for example, sits on Mount Belleview at the headwaters of the East River. Corporations have staked claims four deep next to Mount Emmons on Oh Be Joyful Creek; the Oh Be Joyful runs into the Slate River above Crested Butte. Water from a uranium claim on Fossil Ridge now flows into the Taylor River. There has been approval for another uranium mine on the east side of the basin, and a titanium mine has been proposed on a creek to the south. All these creeks and rivers feed the Gunnison.

* * * * *

Theo Colborn can't let go of the idea that human beings are 96 percent water, and that all of her body's water is from the Gunnison and its tributaries. She is a tall, slender woman with a weathered tan who has begun to explore the effects of over-mineralized water on life, human and otherwise. Colborn used to run a sheep ranch in Hotchkiss, in the agricultural valley west of Crested Butte, across the West Elk Mountains. The North Fork of the Gunnison wound past her ranch. A few years ago, people from the Westmoreland Coal Company, which ran a coal mine nearby, asked her to take stream samples for them. As a part-time pharmacist and full-time environmentalist, she agreed.

Colborn concentrated on cadmium, a trace element found in

the Gunnison Basin's drainage system that has been linked with such human ills as birth defects, hypertension, kidney damage, and bladder and testicular cancer. But she found it hard to measure exactly how much cadmium was entering the aquatic ecosystem, because the concentration fluctuated violently. One day a stream would run high and carry enough dissolved minerals to plate a fish, while the next day the same stream would flow pure. A high mountain thunderstorm might wash down a load of mineral-laden silt, or it might merely dilute the strength of an already mineralized flow. Unless a lab was built at every sampling site in the remote streamsheds, Colborn thought, the sampling results couldn't possibly be useful. What was needed, she decided, was a way to measure what had been in a stream yesterday, or the day before.

At this time Colborn was fifty years old and her children were grown. She left her daughter to run the ranch and moved to Gunnison to attend Western State College, the largest college on the Western Slope, and to involve herself with RMBL. What, she asked in her thesis, sits in the streams for a year or two, absorbing, ingesting, drinking, responding to fluctuations in the flow? Immature insects of the streams, she answered, the stoneflies (*Plecoptera*) known as willow or salmon flies. In their immature state, stonefly larvae inhabit a stream for a couple of years, maturing slowly, shedding an exoskeleton, made up of sugar and protein compounds, now and then, and hibernating in the mud if they haven't managed to mature before winter comes. These exoskeletons provide a reliable witness to every new surge of minerals in the water of the stream, for they are designed as buffers against the weak poisons that sometimes appear in the water, to be sloughed off when necessary.

The worst poisonings kill the insects. An entomologist can gauge the health of a stream merely by looking among the rocks for insects and counting the numbers and species living there. One RMBL entomologist is even pushing a "quick and dirty" way for an untrained staff to test for stream pollution: she has cages of insects lowered into a stream and checked at intervals. If the insects are floating, they're dead, and the water is bad.

Colborn was looking for something more subtle. The most practical approach, she decided, would be to calculate a field concentration factor for each insect and each substance (in this case cadmium), the maximum amount of a given substance that an insect could safely absorb over a given time. That would provide her with a simple constant with which to calculate the actual amount of cadmium that had passed through the stream, even if the actual level in the water at the time of measurement was too low to detect.

In her field-concentration-factor experiment Colborn exposed insects to cadmium-treated water for varying times, then put them in another tank to measure their desorption of the element over time. Finally, she dried and pulverized the insect bodies and measured the cadmium levels. As she plotted the levels, she found they made some bizarre curves on her charts. The insects in the tank didn't lose the cadmium from their bodies; they merely passed it around. There was no desorption factor. The experiment, at first sight, seemed to show her approach to be impractical.

By this stage she was sleeping in her lab, removing and replacing insects from the water tanks at intervals throughout the night. She kept the room cold, around 50 degrees F, because the streams where the insects lived were cold and her budget had no provision for refrigeration. Then one morning she woke up feeling more comfortable than usual—a joker of a fellow student had turned the heat up to 80 degrees F. All her insects had started to molt. She picked up the discarded exoskeletons from the bottom of the tank and in desperation measured their cadmium levels. To her surprise, they were loaded. She tested the water: it was almost cadmium free. She measured the cadmium content of the live insects: there was none. Like iron to a magnet, the cadmium had bound to the discarded skins. The tank had been scoured. She had discovered nature's own streambed Borax.

Cadmium binds with organic matter, she reasoned. Where streams pool, where they pause for an instant before jumping over falls, or where a dogleg creates still water, there will be calmer water where organic matter, like insect corpses, will come to rest.

"This is one of the wonderful things the aquatic insects have apparently been doing for us," Colborn theorizes. "I am sure that over the years there's been a natural weathering and erosion of cadmium into our aquatic systems, but at low levels the insects could cope with it, and they could bind it, molt, and send it to the bottom of the rivers and streams. In mud there is little or no oxygen, so the cadmium that lodges in the bottom becomes fixed. Now of course you could take the cadmium out if you were to expose it to acid."

When Colborn tested untreated water draining from the old Keystone mine above Crested Butte, she found the cadmium load to be seventy parts per billion, seven times the maximum amount allowed in drinking water by government standards. (This was before AMAX's expensive and effective electroclear plant was completed.) But by the time the same water reached the Slate River, the load was only ten to thirty parts per billion. Organic matter like insect skeletons had absorbed the rest. If something happened to release all that cadmium from the organics in the streambed, she thought, the people of the valley would be in trouble. (To her surprise, she found that they might already be in trouble. While no formal studies offering numbers for comparison have been made, she has seen "alarming rates of jaundiced newborn babies, underweight babies, and spontaneous abortions" in the area.)

* * * * *

All that it takes to release minerals into the water is an increase in the acidity of the water, and this does not necessarily come from mining activity. For example, the rains and snows of the Rockies, which until recently were assumed to be untouched by pollution, are now known to be affected by acid rain in the same way as the rains and snows of the Northeast, where acid precipitation has killed the fish in hundreds of lakes. Normally, when clean rain and snow form around fine particles of dust in the atmosphere, they fall to earth as a mild acid, just strong enough to dissolve from the ground the minerals necessary to plant and animal life. Recently, however, RMBL researchers have found far more acid than normal in the rain and snow of the area. In dry winters, when snowfalls are few and far between, the snow that falls is high in concentrated atmospheric pollutants—one hundred times more acid than normal snow, and rising.

Acid rain or snow starts when sulphur and nitrogen oxides are emitted as infinitely small particles from gasoline and diesel engines, and from smokestacks where fossil fuels are burned. When the particles reach the atmosphere they combine chemically with hydrogen ions to form sulphuric and nitric acids. Rain and snow wash these acids to earth. The acidity accumulates—the highest level has been measured after two weeks without any precipitation. In fact, half the acid deposition in the West is in the form of dry fall. The acids trigger a flurry of chemical activity wherever they land, pulling previously fixed minerals into solution because their high positive-ion load demands that ions be exchanged with the minerals in the soil and bedrock with which they come into contact. So minerals are released into surface waters at a rate much faster than nature intended.

Both the acids and the minerals that they release make life at high altitudes precarious for flora and fauna. Trees feel the effects of acid rain first. Needle-leafed trees, like pines and spruces, are usually successful in harsh mountain climates because their many-leafed surfaces capture moisture quickly. But when that water is acid, the waxy protective covering is stripped from the needles, blocking their ability to photosynthesize and exposing them to disease and insect invasion.

On the ground, the acid combines first with organic materials in the soil and leaf litter. The nutrients most needed by plants—calcium, magnesium, and potassium carbonates—combine with the acids first and are leached out of the soil. The regeneration of soil nutrients is blocked, because the microbes in the soil that break down organic matter are killed by the acid. The thin, nutrient-poor mountain soils thus begin to lose what little life-supporting capability they had gained over the long ages. In other areas, when acid precipitation seeps through the soil the acids are neutralized and streams are protected from the acid's direct effects. When acid water flows through most of the soil and rock in the Rockies, little buffering occurs. Instead, minerals are pulled from the surface and combine directly with the water.

When the snow melts in the high country, the runoff is tremendous. The acid accumulations of an entire winter run straight over frozen ground and directly into the streams. No buffering occurs. Fish, who are laying their eggs just as the acids are surging, are particularly vulnerable; a single melt-off can kill an entire generation.

Acid precipitation intensifies the effects of mine drainage. The ferric hydroxide, manganese, cadmium, and other minerals carried by the water in mountain streams form a thick deposit on the rocks, hard as concrete. Acids in the stream release those minerals from the deposit and reload the water with heavy metals. At this point, two things might happen. Either the minerals will be recycled by natural processes and will remove themselves from the water supply by clinging to obstructions in the stream, as they did before. Or the water of many streams will dilute the solution of minerals such that they are no longer as harmful.

While streams are diluting their mineral solutions, though, the process of evaporation is working to concentrate them again, as the dry winds of the Western Slope take up moisture and leave mineral salts behind. The Gunnison River has been dammed again and again. There's the Blue Mesa Reservoir, the Morrow Point Dam, and the Crystal Dam; two additional dams hold up the Gunnison before it reaches its junction with the Colorado. Each dam interrupts the river's natural cleansing processes, and each man-made lake loses gallons of water to evaporation.

* * * * *

While it is true that building a mine in the mountains alters the natural environment, scientists at RMBL have discovered a curious fact: some species flourish with the alteration. Andrew Smith, RMBL researcher and ecologist at the University of Arizona, studies pikas, short-eared relatives of rabbits. Their scientific name is *Ochotona princeps*: little chief. The pika is chief of the rockpile.

Pikas live on talus, and forage in nearby meadows for food. They harvest grass and flowers and carry their harvest back to their talus hideaways, where they neatly stack their booty in bushel-sized piles for consumption during the winter months. Smith has studied pikas the world over; some he has tamed to the point that they answer when he whistles. Among his most curious finds is that pikas thrive on the tailing and overburden from abandoned mines. For pikas, mining has created a new habitat where none existed before.

Another oddity is the broad-leafed sundew (*Drosera rotundifolia*), a plant that thrives in iron bogs—nature's equivalent of an acid mine-drainage pond. Behind Crested Butte, on Mount Emmons, three acidic and highly mineralized springs have flowed for thousands of years, covering 120 acres of the mountainside with reddish deposits of iron oxide, or limonite. One of the springs, less acidic than the others, has pooled where it emerges from the earth and formed an iron bog. In this bog 500 tiny broad-leafed sundews live in an environment that would poison most plants. The sundew has evolved a diet-supplement program: it obtains its food by catching it, using leaves covered with glistening, gland-tipped hairs that secrete a dewy juice that attracts and traps insects.

Bogs like the ones the sundew inhabits have winked in and out of existence for millennia, geologically speaking. Over time the water that pools in the earthen depressions is invaded by plants such as sphagnum moss. The bog eventually fills with so much decayed plant matter that trees begin to grow there. This march from moss to forest, from the simple to the complex, is called ecological succession. But the reverse process can happen, and when it does, it happens rapidly.

When a forest fire was ignited on the mine-construction site on Mount Emmons near the iron bogs, the mountainside slid from forest-level ecology—ecological stage three—back to dust—stage one—in a single day. A graduate student walking the site weeks after the fire accidentally stumbled into an old bog of smoldering peat and severely burned her legs. Where she had disturbed the ground, flames seeped into her footsteps. She was studying under Professor Hugo Ferchau, a plant ecologist from Western State College and RMBL. AMAX, the mining company that owns the burned-over site, had asked Ferchau to try to restore the burn site to stage three—a process that took centuries in nature—within a few years. Speed was essential. The ground was covered with a red powder that repelled moisture when it rained and puffed dust when the wind blew. Each dry summer wind robbed the land; each rain and run-off washed the dirt down to Coal Creek.

Ferchau had to overcome many handicaps: the severe climate, the high winds, the acid soil, the short growing season, the south-facing slope open to desiccation by the blazing sun.

His method of mineland revegetation was to begin by stabilizing the soil and then, using water and nutrients, to give the plant life such a shove that plant and animal communities of increasing diversity would succeed one another speedily, gratefully. Here, he hoped to telescope twenty-five years of ecological succession into three.

Ferchau and his students collected old hay and manure from the ranchers, who were glad to see it hauled away, to spread over the burn. On the road cuts he planted winter rye, a hybrid grass that will not set seed. Rye grows vigorously, stabilizing the slopes. Beneath the protection of the tall grasses, small native grasses find refuge. Wooden shingles beside his seedling spruce protect the trees' tender tips from sunburn when they are exposed by the melting of the snow in the spring. The end product of his labor, a fully mature forest and meadow ecosystem, won't be achieved within his lifetime, but Ferchau, the middle-aged son of a German nurseryman, claims that his AMAX revegetation work is no more complex than the work he and his father did when he was a boy in the Carolinas. High- or low-altitude, plants have simple needs.

The tree seedlings grown at the site prove that altitude alone is not the trouble when revegetating mountain areas. The seedlings germinated well at an altitude of 10,000 feet, deep inside Mount Emmons in the old Keystone mine. In the cave that serves as a greenhouse, bright lights shine hard all through the night and day. The seedlings there sprout higher in six short months than they would after two years of growth outside. Though clearly impractical, it appears that the most efficient way to revegetate high-altitude environments would be to roof over the whole mountain.

* * * * *

The burn sites and road cuts in Ferchau's agenda are child's play compared to the task of trying to revegetate acres of ground-up, chemically treated tailing pond. If a tailing pond isn't planted over it remains a desert, emptying fugitive dust over the valley at the whim of the wind. There have been complaints from areas downwind of AMAX's Climax mine, where tailing ponds have been filling up with dust since early in the century, that the loose dust spreads over the surrounding areas and contaminates the nearby mountain meadows. Particles of molybdenum from these ponds combine with water on the meadows; the molybdenum dissolves and is absorbed by the meadow grasses. If grazing animals—cattle, deer, elk, and mountain sheep in this area—eat too much of the grass, the excess molybdenum will leach the copper from their bodies. A molybdenum-triggered copper shortage that lames and can kill an animal is called molybdenosis.

When the time comes, AMAX will replant these tailing ponds. The AMAX environmental-control engineer, Larry Brown, believes he could probably revegetate anything given a big enough budget. A case in point is a comparatively tiny tailing pond near the newer Henderson mine, the Urad tailing; it cost $7 million in 1974 dollars to turn this small, 125-acre site into a lawn.

The Urad was a molybdenum mine that AMAX purchased for $2 million in 1963. The mine was closed in 1974, leaving 125 acres of bare tailing and a growing season of only twenty frost-free days. At this site, the idea was to lop one hundred years off the natural succession process. First, untreated waste rock was hauled from the new Henderson mine to the tailing. A local lumberyard donated a mulch of wood chips, and truckloads of sewage sludge were hauled up to the divide from Denver. Special batches of high-altitude seeds were planted, and the site was carpeted with dead logs to encourage small animals to move in.

What grows on the site now is what high-altitude ecologist Betty Willard calls an ecological miracle: the former tailing pond is whiskered with four-inch aspen saplings. No one has ever seen an aspen grow from seed here before—not Betty Willard, not Larry Brown. Willard says she's had her graduate students crawl for miles on their hands and knees and they've never found an aspen seedling, not even under an aspen grove—the aspen always come up from root suckers. "But there on that tailing pond," she says, "they've got a whole bunch of aspen seedlings, and we don't know why."

The Urad meadow is long on grass but still short on wildflowers, which take almost as long to mature as trees. Many of the wildflowers of the Gunnison Basin are at least fifty years old, and some are older. The sunflowers live to be over thirty-five, the gentian forty. If a mountain meadow is disturbed, it takes fifty to one hundred years just for the flowers to come back. What's more, there's evidence that each group of mountain plants has adjusted to its surroundings so successfully that, genetically speaking, each valley holds plants that are in some way unique.

* * * * *

Not all of the RMBL's scientists' discoveries can be applied to human problems. Mary Price studies larkspur, a spring flower that bears dark blue blooms on a tall spike. The flowers look like lark's feet. The buds are named *Delphinium nelsonii* for their dolphin-like shape. Price has plots of *Delphinium* all over the upper valley in Gunnison County. Some are on national-forest land near Gothic; others are nearer Crested Butte, on a lot slated for condominium development that will eventually rob Price of five years' work. All of her plots are marked with yellow tags and numbered. Other biologists band birds; Mary Price bands flowers.

Price hand-pollinates her plants. She's an educated bee, harvesting pollen from one larkspur, placing it in one tiny flower, and dusting another with the tip of a toothpick. In the spring she has green knees from crawling through mountain meadows. Several years immersed in larkspur have convinced her that her *Delphinium nelsonii*, were it not a plant, might be considered intelligent. She and her colleague Nicholas Waser have discovered that larkspur has a strategy for keeping its genetic pool well stirred: a plant that is pollinated not by the plant next door, but by more distant neighbors, will set more seeds. Larkspur therefore has a built-in tendency to spread.

Larkspur has evolved a protective system as well as a distributive one. In the Middle Ages, recognizing the plant's enmity to insects, people called it lousewort and used a concoction made of larkspur seeds to exterminate head lice. The chemical substance that did the work was an alkaloid, and the alkaloids produced by the larkspur near Gunnison are slightly different from those produced by the larkspur in Price's Gothic plots. The scientists presume that this may be a fine-tuning of response to differing insect populations in the area.

Larkspur also seems to have worked out an agreement with two other flower species in the valley. There are thousands of individual flowers, but only a limited number of birds and bees to pollinate them. So the flowers bloom in succession, first *Delphinium nelsonii,* then the scarlet gilia, then the taller larkspur, seemingly taking turns in order that each might attract the maximum number of pollinators.

Among those pollinators is the broad-tailed hummingbird, which needs larkspur nectar to survive when it first arrives in the spring. "The broad-tailed hummingbird has the thirst of a drunkard," reports ornithologist William Calder, who has been studying them at RMBL since 1969. "They drink so much nectar they have to bail themselves out." During the day, Calder lurks inside his cabin, keeping an eye out the kitchen window for hummingbirds who stray into his sugar-water lures. The birds he watches for have iridescent red throats and green wings. A swallowtail curve to each wing feather turns the birds' flight into song: the vibrating wingtips make a sound like a carnival top. Calder listens for the whistle, and then like a giant spider lunges for a string that springs a trap. When he has caught a bird, he runs outside with a little beaker to catch the terrified creature's urine, which is essentially recycled nectar. A frightened hummingbird looks as if it just sat in a dewdrop. It takes three or four catches before Calder's beaker is full enough to run his experiment. He is trying to figure out how a bird that lives on nectar stays healthy.

Calder's respect for his half-pint subjects comes from years of intimacy: he was the scientist who discovered that hummingbirds keep exacting hours. They always awaken half an hour before sunrise—that's sunrise by the almanac, even though sunrise in the valley where the birds nest may be as late as 10 A.M. Sometimes a hummingbird is confined to her nest, keeping the eggs warm during a thunderstorm. Her food intake that day is curtailed, and she doesn't drink enough calorific nectar to warm herself and her eggs all night. When that happens, she puts herself on hold, lowering her governor and stopping all her metabolic functions. She cools down like a hibernator. Half an hour before sunrise, she begins to wake up. Her heart begins to beat faster, her temperature rises, and she readies herself for breakfast with the sun, as usual. Calder would like to know what awakens her. He discovered her nighttime coma by seeding hummingbird nests with tiny electronic heat sensors disguised as eggs. The bird obligingly incubated the sensor for him. If she noticed that she was sitting on a machine, he couldn't tell.

Calder banded one hummingbird at Gothic and recaptured it eight years later. That meant eight migrations, sixteen trips to and from Mexico's Sierra Madre, and always a return to the same backyard of the same ghost town in Colorado.

"That's all done on a fiftieth of an ounce of brain," Calder marvels. "Sometimes it's hard to distinguish between what's science and what's just emotional awe."

Calder once saw a sparrowhawk's food cache: three dead mice and a dead hummingbird hooked neatly to a strip of barbed wire fencing. He was relieved to discover that the hummingbird, with no band on its foot, was a stranger. He once saved the life of a hummingbird who had a dried and encrusted bumblebee jammed so tightly over her beak that she was starving to death, unable to open her mouth. Calder, curious, took out his electronic gadgets and measured the force necessary to drive a hummingbird beak through a bee body. It had apparently been a mid-air collision, with the hummingbird cruising blind at over twenty-five miles an hour.

* * * * *

The hummingbird's need for larkspur nectar for its survival is an example of coevolution, a term invented by Paul Ehrlich, professor of Population Biology at Stanford University. He defines coevolution as the reciprocal evolution of two or more ecologically intimate species. The term was coined in order to explain the plant-animal interactions he was observing at RMBL in his studies of butterflies.

In the late 1960s, in the flush of his first forays into the newly minted science of coevolution, Ehrlich received funding for an extensive study of the pink lupine (*Lupinus amplus*) and the flower's chief predator, the little blue butterfly (*Glaucopsyche lygdamus*). He was looking for ways in which the predator and prey adjusted to one another—one more aspect of coevolution.

Ehrlich hired three helpers, and he had a full-time technician back at Stanford doing gas chromatography on the plant's juices. After three years they determined that the little blue butterfly did indeed affect the lupine, and strongly: the butterflies destroyed 75 percent of the flowers that the plants put out. Ehrlich also began to suspect that natural selection had caused the plants to flower earlier than they ought, so that they could set seeds before the butterflies arrived. The general conclusion was valid; but after all the effort, the results were not very satisfying.

Then, in 1969, Gothic suffered an unusually heavy and late snowstorm in June. Snow fell for three days. The lupines froze and died in the cold, wet snow. The little blue butterflies, their food source destroyed, disappeared from the valley, not to be seen again until recently. The plants, perennials, could easily sacrifice a year's production of seeds in exchange for the demise of their enemy. Because of a freak snowstorm, Ehrlich learned more than he had been able to learn in three summers of meticulous research. Although the study hasn't been revived, Ehrlich still keeps an eye out for the little blues. He theorizes that now, in a more benign, predator-free environment, the lupine might eventually bloom again in the area.

"People keep trying to manipulate the size of populations of other organisms," he says. "Either they're trying to maximize a population, as in a harvest, or they want to suppress a pest. Knowing how a population changes in nature, and why, is vitally important to knowing how to regulate population size. We need to know how to do our manipulations safely. For example, the way people have thought about pest insects is all wrong. They think that once they know what the pest species is, they can determine the best control measure. They can't. Every population, within a species, has a different ecology."

Ehrlich personally witnessed one attempt at butterfly population control that backfired while in Trinidad studying butterflies that feed on passion fruit flowers. Farmers in the area were trying to cultivate passion vines as a cash crop. Another butterfly, not Ehrlich's pet species, was attracted to the commercial crop in such numbers that it became a nuisance. Ehrlich remembers that the vines were doused with pesticides, and yet the problem became worse. The reason was coevolutionary. Passion vines contain lethal alkaloids. The butterflies, having coevolved with the vines, were used to handling the poisons, and they quickly became resistant. Ants, on the other hand, were susceptible to the poisons, and it was predatory ants that normally kept the population of passion fruit butterflies in check.

Ehrlich usually wears his lepidopterist's hat and a fisherman's vest, fully pocketed at every seam. He slings a stick with a bag at its end over his shoulder—his net. The effect is that of a hobo who has wandered too far from the railroad track. At any moment Ehrlich is likely to interrupt his walk to lurch off the path in chase of a butterfly—a little blue, a tiger swallowtail, a checkerspot. He makes his catches with a graceful sweep climaxed by a flick of the wrist: after thirty-five years, Ehrlich is an excellent netman.

Ehrlich is most interested in catching the checkerspot (*Euphydryas editha*), a medium-sized butterfly whose wings are patterned in rich spots of brown and bronze. The ones he catches in Gothic are the same species as, though very dissimilar to, the checkerspots he has studied for two decades at Jasper Ridge, Stanford University's biological reserve. His checkerspot studies represent the largest, longest-running insect studies anyone has conducted anywhere in the world. He has found that three different populations of checkerspots lived on Jasper Ridge: same species, same area, but different habitats. Since he began observing their habits, one of the three populations on Jasper Ridge has disappeared. The other two are flourishing. He's now surveying populations of checkerspots and other butterflies in all the mountain ranges of the Great Basin.

In effect, each Great Basin mountain range is a nature reserve. The butterfly populations have been separated from one another for 10,000 years, since the retreat of the Wisconsinian glaciers transformed the mountains into temperate islands in a sea of desert. The surveys Ehrlich makes of the butterflies in the Gothic area will become the example of butterfly life in a non-island, or continental, habitat. He's doing this partly because he believes that if we really want to maintain the diversity of species on earth we'd better figure out how nature reserves work. His studies in the Great Basin mountains have led him to discover an ironic fact: the best way to *decrease* species diversity in a region is to make an island of it.

"It's one of the pressing questions today," Ehrlich explains. "If you are going to try to save the diversity of organisms in the world, what size and shape and arrangement should you make nature reserves?" There is almost no information on how to design nature reserves if you want to maintain things like insects and little herbaceous plants. Most of what has been done has been done on large animals.

"The number of organisms in any area is a balance between two factors: what feeds diversity in, and what feeds diversity out. In the long range, evolution and migration feed diversity in. In both the long and short range, extinction removes diversity. In the short range, you just have migration and extinction. What happens when you isolate an area? If you suddenly make a square mile around Gothic an island by mowing down everything outside of it, what happens? Migration to the island is reduced, and extinction is increased."

As he answers his own question, Ehrlich pauses to snap his net over a struggling *Glaucopsyche lydgamus*, his old friend from the lupine study. "For some species, the island would be too small, and the population would crash. For others, the island would include only part of their habitat, which would not be big enough to maintain the population. So what you'd have is a so-called relaxation, or collapse, of the flora and fauna. This is something most people don't realize. If you set aside a nature reserve, the first thing that happens is that the number of species it maintains collapses from its previous height to a new equilibrium level, established by a new rate of in-migration and a new rate of extinction."

But Ehrlich believes that while preservation in natural reserves may be an imperfect response, it is also the best response. "The importance of endangered species is as symbols of what's going on," he says. "Endangered species are to protect areas. This area ought to be protected." He makes an emphatic gesture with his butterfly net. The net encompasses the valley, as if he were capturing all that lives there and holding it, protected, still fluttering.

* * * * *

The Gunnison Basin is cut off from the rest of Colorado by high, snowy mountains. There is some evidence that the basin has been isolated, a biogeographical island surrounded by a sea of mountains and therefore unique, for thousands of years. There is a theory that the seed stock of the plants living in this area was established long ago, by the survivors of the last Ice Age. RMBL researcher Joseph Barrell, who proposed this theory in his book *Flora of the Gunnison Basin*, visited the basin throughout the 1950s, when disturbance in the area was at a low ebb.

Barrell postulated that the glaciers of 10,000 years ago forced the plants of the Gunnison Basin into a small central area of lowest altitude. All of the higher lands were snow covered and inclement to life all year round, but the valley lies in an area that was not thoroughly blanketed with the continental glacier. All but the most adaptive species perished, Barrell believed, and this explains why the same sorts of plants are found throughout the basin, transecting ecological zones, from the low deserts to the high alpine tundra. Barrell wrote that they grew out from the center with the melting of the snow.

"For at the end of the period of glaciation, as the snowfields and the glaciers began to inch back from their greatest advance, the hardy, compact flora at the center must also have inched back with equal speed," Barrell wrote. "It seems to me that the pressure to repopulate from the center must have been explosive, and that the present plant population of the Gunnison Basin must substantially be an expansion of the former population at the center."

Many people who have lived there agree that the area is special, although there hardly seems a mountain region in the world that doesn't have its loyal boosters. Professor Barrell himself believed that the basin's uniqueness had a lot to do with the well-rooted stability of the plant life in the basin. Tramping the entire area, he surveyed the numbers of plants, as well as identifying their species. By his count, only 5 percent of the plant species in the basin were invaders from other continents. This is a small number, for it is considered that 18 percent of the wildlife species in the northeastern United States have been introduced from other countries. Barrell surmised that invaders have historically fared poorly in the Gunnison Basin because the native species had already made full use of the ecological niches that existed there: foreign species would invade but remain unable to colonize in this fully exploited region.

This is not to say that the region cannot change. Mining, grazing, irrigation, changes in water quality and quantity, human settlements—all have disturbed the existing balance of life in the Gunnison Valley. Some incursions, like the large mining operation and dams, are impossible to ignore; others are more subtle.

Joseph Barrell wrote that he found the largest numbers of plant invaders around areas that had been disturbed in such a way that new habitats for adventurous foreigners had been opened. Dandelions are the most common example. The dandelion is a European flower that now flourishes in Gothic, although it didn't in the days of the silver boom. Today, dandelions mark the spots where RMBL professors have held their nature-study classes out on the meadow. Where the classes were held, the dandelions flourish, outnumbering native species ten to one.

CHAPTER TWO

The Bulldozer at the Door

THE little Colorado town of Crested Butte has heaved with mining boom and mining bust since the day it was founded. Born in the silver boom of 1880, it was incorporated in the back room of the Elk Avenue drugstore, then one of only a few wooden buildings poking up over a city of tents. The town served as the supply depot for the soon-to-be-ghost towns of Floresta, Gothic, Irwin, and Elkton, raw mining camps that flourished briefly and then died away. For one uproarious season, in 1882, two thousand people strolled up and down Elk Avenue.

It was a high point for Crested Butte, and the crowds evaporated almost as quickly as they had appeared. For decades the town never outgrew the plan imposed on it in its frontier heyday: the old town is eight blocks long by eight wide, large enough to accommodate people when the mines were flourishing, small enough that people could keep an eye on things when the mines went bust. Crested Butte sits square to the freestanding mountain of the same name, overlooking a wide green mile of valley-bottom pasture. For many years it just sat quietly in the lap of Mount Emmons, the Red Lady.

Before her death in November 1985, Mary Yelenick lived with her husband, Frank, beside their liquor store on Elk Avenue. Mary was a retired schoolteacher. She ran the store and looked after Frank, who had been disabled in a mining accident in 1947. The Yelenicks, like their neighbors the Somraks, the Perkos, and the Yaklichs, were miners and children of miners,

miners who had come to Crested Butte from Slovakia just after the turn of the century. Most of the men had earned their pay underground regularly until 1952, when they were all told abruptly that Colorado Fuel and Iron, which owned the Big Mine and its coal, was shutting down. Then the Denver and Rio Grande Railroad, which for seventy years had ferried coal down the valley, followed suit. Many miners were forced to leave town, salvaging what they could. One man sold two fully furnished homes to an Oklahoman looking for a hunting camp for only $1,600.

Mary Yelenick was short and round, and she protected her housedress with a printed apron that enveloped her from chin to knees. In the old days, when a customer stepped into the Crested Butte liquor store a bell rang in her home, and in a few moments she would be in the store, smoothing her apron with her hands. Her hair was gray and held down in the back with hairpins. She used to fiddle with them while she talked. After the Big Mine closed, she remembered, she and Frank watched time go by from their storefront on Elk Avenue, fifty-two Saturday-night polkas a year. A new mine, the Keystone, came in on the side of Mount Emmons in 1955, and a mining mill was built there to process the gold, silver, copper, lead, and zinc that came out of the mine. But that vein petered out in only a dozen years, and the Keystone—like the Big Mine and the many silver mines before it—closed down.

Mining is a risky business. It can make people rich, and it can leave a legacy of casualties, not all of them human. Coal Creek was one such casualty. Coal Creek runs through Crested Butte in a gulch half as wide as a city street and deep enough to hide in. It starts ten miles west of town, at the site of the Irwin ghost town. The 1880 architects of Crested Butte, who took the plan that was used for Colorado Springs and laid it over their own townsite, disregarded the creek, which slices the plan like a crack in a windowpane. It comes rolling down from Irwin, meets the town at the corner of Whiterock Avenue and First Street, crosses Elk Avenue's main drag at Second Street, and exits at Fourth and Teocali. Though it crosses eight streets on the way, only five are bridged. Up until the 1950s, people could step out their back doors and catch dinner in the creek. It was a blue river trout stream, with rainbow trout, Eastern brook trout, and brown trout.

The Keystone put an end to that. Its tailing pond, which contained the waste rock and chemicals after the ore had been milled, was built upstream of Coal Creek. Dissolved lead, cadmium, zinc, and manganese washed right into the creek, and the fish were wiped out.

Coal Creek was one casualty. The valley's ponderosa pine was another. In 1877, Howard M. Smith, the town's first mayor, built a sawmill to make strong beams to support the mineshafts that were beginning to pockmark the mountains. The best wood was ponderosa, which grew just below town in the East River valley, just where the bluffs begin to plump out of the flat alluvium like earthen pillows. These big-tree groves are now gone from the valley. They never grew back, and without the trees to hold it back, soil fled downhill with the spring runoff. Up to twenty feet of soil has disappeared since the trees were stripped out, and sagebrush covers the ground.

Despite their losses, people in Crested Butte saw mining as the one thing that kept the town alive; the rich seams of bituminous and anthracite coal knit into the complex geology around the town kept them hoping. Anything lost was just the price of progress. To the old-timers, who dated all their tales with reference to the closing of this or that mine, trading minerals for food and clothing and housing was good, right, and proper. "Everything good comes from the earth," they would say. "Other people just massage our minerals and make them into different shapes. This is where everything begins."

A town like Crested Butte, some 9,000 feet above sea level,

trades its natural resources for goods from the outside. Farming is impossible; the growing season goes by in 36 days. A few coldframes in town produce lettuce and radishes, and people in town admire one transplanted Pennsylvanian who yearly and with great effort grows edible tomatoes. The Ute Indians who hunted Crested Butte's sheltered East River Valley wintered elsewhere. They sought the summer abundance of elk in the valley and fled from the winter snow. In Crested Butte, the snow can accumulate to three or four hundred inches; it demands reckoning.

Householders shovel their roofs after snowfalls so their homes won't collapse. Biweekly blizzards are common any time between October and June. There are winters when the snow is so deep that people lift their shovels high in order to throw the snow off the roofs. In the bars they laugh about a man who spent an entire afternoon shoveling the roof over his back room only to find he had missed his house entirely and was clearing out his back yard. Crested Butte is the home of the two-story outhouse. It's not pleasant after the thaw, but in January at least people can find it. For the most part, the ground produces rocks. Rocks under the streets wait for the spring thaw in June, when they extrude from ruts and interfere with traffic. The rocks hidden more deeply in the ground hold the minerals. These rocks lure the miners, and they always will.

Then, in the 1960s, everything began again. Newcomers arrived, and they saw a different future for Crested Butte. They looked to the northwest and saw magic mountains. This alarmed the old-timers, who had always called them the West Elks. The newcomers wore scruffy jeans and smoked marijuana, and they scared the old-timers half to death.

"They looked fierce," Mary Yelenick recalled. "I was afraid of them, because we had all heard those things out in California, those murders. They'd come here and stay a few weeks and then they'd disappear." The old-timers mistrusted these transients, who would appear one morning to buy milk at Stefanik's grocery, lay a sleeping bag in the back of an abandoned woodshed or in a broken-down vehicle, and then vanish when the weather changed. It didn't improve matters when the "kids" started renting houses and staying in town.

At that time the population of the town was about 200, most of whom Frank and Mary had grown up with. They all attributed the influx of transients to the new ski area that was being developed two miles north of town at the base of Crested Butte Mountain. While they were glad of the business for their store, having these strangers as neighbors was another story.

"Eventually I liked those kids," Mary Yelenick said. "I learned they were human beings. One day some girl stopped in and asked me over to fix an old machine they had in the Company Store [a gallery of tiny shops next door to the Yelenicks' liquor store]. I went over and found out they were just like my own children. I'm so glad I got an opportunity to meet them, because I was never afraid again."

Other folks had a harder time adjusting, and the newcomers had some doubts of their own about the old-timers. The new immigrants had looked long and hard for a place where progress seemed to have stopped: they stayed in Crested Butte precisely because it seemed the one place in the United States that hadn't yet shaken hands with the twentieth century. The town had rare treasures to offer. There were the original 1880 storefronts still intact. Crested Butte was a place where time seemed to pause, ponder, even stand still. But more important was the isolation, the mountains and the wildlife, the silence, and the long views of empty space lifting toward spruce forests, tundra, granite, and snow. The newcomers had turned their backs on cities. Crested Butte was a place to begin again.

No one realized, however—neither the old-timers nor the newcomers—how vulnerable this mountain idyll was. Crested Butte was no different from other towns that in the 1970s found themselves growing so fast and becoming so tough that truckers went out of their way to spend the night elsewhere. Scenery, minerals, oil, and snow in the Rockies were drawing outsiders by the thousands to small, down-at-the-heel mining and cattle towns just like this one. All up and down the Rockies people were waiting for the new boom. National forests were full of exploration geologists seeking molybdenum, titanium, uranium, and a score of other minerals. Whole mountains were being certified skiable. In the valley bottoms, cattle were stumbling over wooden pegs with red plastic flags that marked projected housing developments. A lot of small towns were being swallowed up so quickly they never felt the teeth.

The twentieth century finally struck Crested Butte in 1977, when a vast new molybdenum field was discovered on Mount Emmons, just a few miles from town and next to the old Keystone site: The old-timers saw a dream come true. This would be the biggest mine the county had ever seen. More people would work there than lived in Crested Butte.

The newcomers, on the other hand, were appalled at the changes the new mine would bring. They had staked their future on keeping this pokey little Colorado town the way it was.

* * * * *

One of the newcomers Mary Yelenick liked very much was Don Bachman, a rangy, deep-voiced San Franciscan who smokes cigarettes without filters, down to the end. He owns five plaid woolen shirts and is sure to be wearing one of them any time between October and May. When Bachman came to Crested Butte in 1965, his head was so hairy people couldn't tell back from front, unless they looked for his glasses. He came to work the ski patrol at the then-tiny ski area and found a town with dirt streets, dusty in the summer and rutted in the spring. He found a main street that hadn't changed since the late nineteenth century, the last time there was any money in the town. He found that in the winter he could reach town by taking a dogsled from Aspen, 25 miles to the northwest over Paradise Divide. The place smelled of smoke from wood and coal stoves. When he looked up he saw the flat plate of the horizon miles away, heaped up with scoops of snowy mountain in every direction except the one he had come from. So he stayed.

By 1967 Bachman was a part of the community. He married, settled down, and bought Tony's Tavern. Tony's was an old-timer hangout at the time, and under another name it still is, though the old-timers are older now and confine their appointments with the bar to the afternoons. Bachman put $1,500 in Tony's pocket and took over, but even with a loyal clientele he and his wife struggled. Despite his efforts to immerse himself in local politics and business, the trust of the older residents ran no deeper than Coal Creek in September.

In 1971 Bachman gave up on Tony's. He left town and didn't come back for four years. By then the town was growing rapidly; the bar he had bought for $1,500 sold for $50,000, and empty lots were sprouting condominiums. What Bachman called "intelligent hippies" were beginning to roll in: the only holes in their jeans were those worn by fat wallets in their back pockets. The old-timers made no such distinction: to them, hair was hair and newcomers were newcomers.

To Jim Kuziak, who arrived in 1971, there was a big difference. "We were too straight for the people we replaced," Kuziak says. "If you did any kind of work, they thought you were a jerk. Now we look at the people who work eight to five and we say, the jerks are ruining the place." Kuziak is a farmer's son from Pennsylvania. He has blue eyes and white skin that flushes to ruddy when he gets angry, which he often does. A registered architect and landscape architect, he became the Gunnison County Planner in 1975, a position in which he discovered that his temper's shortest fuse was with developers. But when Kuziak came to Crested Butte, the first thing he did was to buy buildings in the old town and develop them. "I was following my father's advice: to walk in the other guy's shoes before you criticize him," he explains. He came to town to escape success. He had been the designer of the metro stations in Atlanta's new subway system, and he had worked in New York. "I sat in all these firms and saw all these guys with alcoholic wives and kids in private schools, and all this stuff, and two weeks' vacation. Seeing where they were going, that was nowhere to go." Jim was twenty-seven at the time.

"There was a real rub between the new- and the old-timers," Kuziak recalls. "I think that it was the key to making this place work and to making it unique." The lady who ran the restaurant on Elk and Fourth, for example, refused to let any of the newcomers in her place. This went on until Miles Arber, who had purchased the *Crested Butte Chronicle* and was happily playing at being an editor, came in with the headline, "Mrs. B. finally serves longhairs." The subheading was, "Today Johnny Somrak found one in his soup." The lady sued.

But what really turned the town over, in Kuziak's opinion, was the fight for the town council. The Grubstake Saloon on Elk Avenue's main business block had been purchased by four new-timers. Seeking what they considered beautification, the four tacked a wooden porch and walk on the front of the Grubstake. With its swinging doors, the saloon looked like something out of Dodge City. The new-timers liked it; the old-timers didn't. The city council flexed its zoning ordinances and made them tear it out. The Grubstake lost its porch and the newcomers lost patience.

The city fathers had misjudged their opponents. They saw people like Don Bachman, who would lock up his bar and go vacationing whenever he got some extra cash, and from this lackadaisical business attitude they inferred that the new-timers would be easy to pressure. What the old-timers couldn't see was their political sophistication. Crested Butte had become the happy hunting ground for veterans of the 1960s underground revolution. They were tired of fighting, but they hadn't forgotten how. They were, to name a few, a New York University law school graduate who had been organizing Mexicans in Denver; a retired Nader's raider; an MIT Ph.D. in physics who had left the Air Force in protest against the MX; and a Manhattan lawyer who considered himself lucky to get out of New York alive. Don Bachman remembers it as huge deposits of creativity waiting for an event.

If the old-timers had been reasonable about it, Kuziak feels, Crested Butte would have slowly gotten some newcomers on the town council and the place would have puttered along, maintaining the status quo. "But as it was, the four who owned the Grubstake said, 'We've had enough. We're going to get everyone registered to vote and get all our own people elected.' We got a whole council elected with all freaks on board. There was shock value there," Kuziak recalls.

"My whole theory of planning was to come here where there was no corruption," he continues. "There was no funny business because there was nothing worth funny business. You could play at whatever you wanted. If you wanted to be a planner, you played at being a planner. If you wanted to run a newspaper, you could buy it for $5,000 and run it, and show up if you wanted, and if you didn't want to print it, who cared? We got to play at running a town, and do something a little different than dealing with the power structure, the money structure, and the politics, because no one cared. We got to do some unique playing around."

* * * * *

Most communities are swept along by time and call it progress; Crested Butte made time an ally and called it controlled growth. Within three years after the Grubstake confrontation, the town had passed strict architectural controls to keep out trailer parks and A-frames. The controls have kept the place a living, working town. The town converted to home rule, which gave it increased autonomy from the state. It became certified as a National Historic District, further protecting it from inappropriate development. Kuziak transferred to the county seat, where he drafted a county land-use plan more to Crested Butte's liking.

Crested Butte was not, in all this, a typical Rocky Mountain town. Most places welcome growth. Small-town people who are born and raised in the same place and remember their grandparents' stories of the frontier see economic growth coming to their communities and can't wait to install aluminum siding and buy a new Maytag. But the new town government in Crested Butte was full of people who had seen the other side of the coin, and they were saying, No thanks. They came to Crested Butte because it sits at the head of a magnificent valley on the way to nowhere, with no interstate passing through. Crested Butte was isolated because of the mountains, and because of the weather it stayed that way. The town's location graced it with several years' respite before ski developers, highway developers, and mining developers arrived, all to follow Will Rogers's advice: "Buy land. They're not making it any more."

At this point development was only just beginning to eat up the valley. Between the suburban housing tracts in Gunnison County there still existed patches of grassy serenity. On an early fall morning the ranchers would be out on their horses, herding cattle down the highway. The Western mystique was there—the seductive power of open space, independence, and elbow room. The ranchers, who owned much of the valley, were still in control.

"Ranching power has always been the power around here," says Jim Kuziak. "I'd much rather see the control in the ranchers' hands than in the tourists' fickle hands or in the mining interests' hands. Ranchers have visions. They're philosophers who do different things all day long, being businessmen, veterinarians, agronomists. You get a good rancher and you've got the best."

But the ranchers were besieged. A third of the ranches in the county had disappeared in the last twenty-five years. Beef prices hadn't kept up with inflation, and the receipts from hay and cattle sales had gone down. When a developer offered to buy land from a rancher who was barely staying alive and paid for a residential tax assessment rather than an agricultural assessment, he was seldom refused. Even if the rancher hung on to his land, the people and dogs and snow machines overran the pastures and scared pounds off the herds. Agriculture is labor intensive, and hired hands don't get rich. One rancher told a Colorado Department of Agriculture researcher, "When the mine went in, my son quit putting up our hay for $3.50 an hour and went to work in the mine for $8.50 an hour. I had to buy $100,000 worth of machinery to put up $15,000 worth of hay." The farmer feeds us all, but can't afford his own beef. For Colorado farms and ranches, an average investment of half a million dollars yields a 1.3 percent return.

Ninety percent of the privately owned land in Gunnison County is ranchland. Every acre that stays that way helps maintain the quality of life in the valley. Kuziak figures that if you keep the land committed to ranching, most other things will maintain themselves. He drafted a county land-use plan that seeks to do that. One of his first acts as county planner was to toss out the jumble of zoning maps and ordinances he found. "They had zoned by putting a map up in the bank and saying, 'Now everyone come in and color what it is you want it to be.' They had avalanche slopes on national-forest land zoned for high-density housing. It was ludicrous."

Gunnison County's land-use plan is unique in the state. "We came up with a bunch of about twenty Ma-and-apple-pie values," said Kuziak. "Things like maintaining the ranchers, maintaining the air quality, maintaining the recreation values, respecting the rights of present landowners. Making growth pay its own way."

Kuziak and the other people who are working to maintain the quality of life in the valley are not mountain people. The old-timers are the closest to mountain people that the upper valley has ever seen. Yet in this peculiar time when everything loose in the country was sliding toward central Colorado, being a mountain person was a state of mind. A couple of years ago a University of Colorado professor of mountain ecology had two visitors from Thailand. These men were interested in the development of their own mountains; the professor brought them to Crested Butte to give them a taste of ours. They spent the day in conference with the town mayor and his council, who told them about the perils of development and uncontrolled growth. As they were leaving, one of the visitors turned to the professor and very politely thanked him, saying, "I am very happy to have the opportunity to see that the problems you have with your mountain tribes are quite similar to ours."

The people who lived in Crested Butte had the zeal of converts. But they were not actually mountain people; they were scenery people, and they just wanted to keep other people out of their view.

"The first time I was elected," said former mayor Tommy Glass, who gained a council seat in 1972, "the main issue was gaining control of our destiny as a community. I ran on a platform of more stringent zoning and architectural controls, and my first issue after I was elected was establishing a historic district in Crested Butte. But the real issue was one of local authority, the community gaining control over its future, people having an opportunity to really decide what it is they want to do as a community."

Determination to control their own destiny taught people in town an endless lesson in systematic ecology. They were discovering that in order to keep the town the way they liked it, passing ordinances containing cosmetic architectural controls was not enough. They were going to have to control growth and development in the entire East River Valley.

Former mayor Tommy Glass said, "I think the critical thing about reactions to growth in Crested Butte was that we were a community. People were willing to knock themselves out in order to see things happen properly, in order to control their own destiny." Glass remembers that, "They thought we were insane, and we were. Crazy like foxes. ... We grabbed all the power we could." Today the town, tomorrow the county. Glass and his cronies were night riders on the growth-control patrol. One local battle for controlled growth reached nationwide and sent tremors through President Ford's 1976 reelection campaign. It was Crested Butte's first taste of the big time. Bo Calloway, a Georgian who served as Ford's campaign manager in 1975, had purchased the faltering Crested Butte ski area in 1971. He soon applied for a permit from the U.S. Forest Service to expand the ski area to another mountain, called Snodgrass (named for an early forest ranger). Through four years of analysis and study, as the Forest Service slowly processed his request, Calloway served in the U.S. government as Secretary of the Army. He kept his investment alive by building and improving the condominiums and lodges in the ski area. He had already incorporated his ski area as Mount Crested Butte when he heard that his application to the Forest Service had been tentatively denied. Glass and others in Crested Butte were relieved. Expansive ski development in the valley would have trumped their bid for destiny.

Ski booms are real-estate booms. Speculators, who have no intention of living in a community, buy the town's land. The first speculator makes a killing and ten more follow, all trying to buy low and sell high. The prices of buildings balloon, bringing up the prices of the lots next door. So the next speculator skips the lot next door and buys land farther on down the road. Presto! A strip city springs up. Developers play leapfrog across all the available lots in the valley. There goes the neighborhood, and your old friends can't afford to live there anymore. But in Crested Butte, people were more interested in making a living than in making a killing.

"It seemed to me that the town was formed to circumvent county land-use regulations," Glass reports. "Most of the county was about to be designated under Colorado House Bill 1041, which is natural hazards identification. The whole area is built on mancos shale." Mancos shale is porous between its layers. Under pressure, entire sections of shale will slide upon one another when they're wet. During spring runoff, they're wet all the time. "I can show you one house that slid off its foundations three times because of the shale," Glass continues. "There is one condominium project that moved so much when the shale got wet one spring that it ripped its gas lines out of the ground. This is the kind of land Mount Crested Butte owned, and they wanted to be sure the county didn't zone it for hazards identification, because Bo Calloway was in the land business. They obviously couldn't make money selling lift tickets."

For that matter, while this fact is overlooked by Glass, neither the ski runs of Mount Crested Butte nor those of many older ski areas in the state were designed with environmental considerations in mind. Cutting a swath of vegetation off a mountainside changes the rates of water percolation and runoff and silts up the neighboring streams. But topsoil wasn't Glass's point: "Mount Crested Butte was a big problem for us because, all of a sudden, here was a town that didn't give a damn about anything in terms of responsible development, and the town was controlled entirely by the major developer and his employees."

The matter ended when two significant events occurred. On new information from Calloway's development company, the Forest Service tentatively agreed to reconsider granting the

Snodgrass expansion permit. Second, the district ranger, whose decision it would be to grant the permit, was transferred to Durango and replaced by a man whose last assignment had been in Calloway's native Georgia. Mayor Glass came up smoking. He, County Judge Levin (who had been one of the four owners of the Grubstake Saloon), and Miles Arber, editor of the *Crested Butte Chronicle,* cried foul all the way to Democratic Senator Floyd Haskell's office in Denver. A Senate investigation eventually cleared Calloway of charges of using his Secretary of the Army post to buy influence with the Forest Service, but he was forced to resign from the Ford campaign. Ford lost. Carter won. Crested Butte got a taste of the big time and the Snodgrass ski area has yet to be built.

Ex-Mayor Glass and his friends had seen no reason not cause trouble. Their banners said things like "environment" and "carrying capacity," and Calloway was a rock in the path of righteousness. Even without the ski expansion the valley was already getting crowded—the town of Crested Butte was growing about 20 percent a year. People were foraging ten miles into the national forest for dead wood, when a couple of years before there had been plenty of wood within two miles. Now the town had a new sewage-treatment plant, at great expense, and was studying a new cistern system. They had to hire a whole sequence of dog catchers. Up the road, Mount Crested Butte was growing, across the road Crested Butte was growing, and down south was a Crested Butte South. When it came to the new homes, the county's income and expenses didn't match. For example, $5,000 was spent on snow removal for the people in a little cluster of houses three miles up the road toward Paradise Drive. They contributed only $2,000 to the county in taxes. Jim Kuziak, who lived out that way, called it the "last house in town" syndrome. Growth didn't pay for itself where he lived, but the place belonged to his girlfriend's parents.

Traffic got worse and the roads more rutted; each new condominium required both electric baseboards for heat and a woodstove for atmosphere. Mount Crested Butte had expanded its resort and now advertised 4,000 pillows, which each morning translated into 4,000 flushes.

Still. Still, in Crested Butte you could leave the country, your door unlocked, and come back home to find things the way you left them. People still dropped by the Crested Butte Liquor Store to see if Mary Yelenick needed her roof shoveled. The only violent crimes were those committed by stray dogs on one another. The town was still eight blocks long by eight blocks wide, and there were a few empty storefronts on Elk Avenue. Heaving and yawing, the plan still worked.

But there was one impact the county and town couldn't control. Ranchers and private owners comprise only 15 percent of the county. The other 85 percent is owned by the citizens of the United States under the auspices of the federal government and overseen by the U.S. Forest Service, the Bureau of Land Management, and the National Park Service. Forest Service land is maintained in the national interest. The entrance sign says, "Welcome to Gunnison National Forest. Land of Many Uses." Here are some of the uses the Forest Service allows: it leases grazing land to ranchers; it allows ski runs to be built on Crested Butte Mountain; it leases forest land to lumberers, although not always with the approval of the town of Crested Butte; it encourages hikers and backpackers in the summer and cross-country skiers in the winter, all of whom at some time wander into town looking for sandwiches and bathrooms; in the fall it encourages elk hunting. Crested Butte's economy depends on these enterprises. People come to town, spend a little money, and go home.

The Forest Service encourages another use. Minerals are fair game on public lands. According to the General Mining Law of 1872, a law that was written to encourage grizzled prospectors with burros, any miner who finds a marketable deposit on public land is free to stake a claim, use the land above and adjoining the deposit, dig out the ore, and sell it.

* * * * *

In 1977, in the same issue as it modestly reported its nomination for a Pulitzer Prize, the *Chronicle* reported that "A major molybdenum effort is being slated for the Crested Butte area sometime in the indefinite but not too distant future." The information that American Metals Climax, Inc. (AMAX) had claimed a $7 billion molybdenum deposit in Mount Emmons, two miles above town, came to the *Chronicle* through a friend of the editor's in Wyoming, who had heard it from the president of the U.S. Energy Corporation. "Despite the apparently deliberate efforts to maintain a very low profile and cloak in secrecy the efforts of AMAX to do its core drilling in the vicinity," the *Chronicle* reported, "it has become increasingly well known that this kind of exploratory effort has been going on." Many area residents just had to step out their back doors to see a pair of lights twinkling near the top of Mount Emmons from the tip of the AMAX drilling rig.

Just over 12,000 people lived in Gunnison County. The prospect of a large mine pleased most of them, for they saw it as a good way for the county to draw money and jobs. The population of Crested Butte itself was about 1,200. A couple of hundred old-timers liked the idea of a mine. "Great," they said. "After all, you can't eat scenery." But what the majority of the town wanted to know was, What is this AMAX? And what is molybdenum, anyway?

Miners call it moly. It is an effective steel and iron hardener that melts at 4,730 degrees F; iron melts at 2,795 degrees F. Alloyed with iron, moly adds strength, toughness, wear resistance, corrosion resistance, and efficiency. It is used in knives, jet engines, missiles, automobiles, arctic pipelines, railroad tracks, and ten-speed bicycles. Moly is the legacy of giant pre-Cambrian crustal stretches that took place over 600 million years ago in an area traversing Colorado from the northeast to the southwest, forming extensive fractures in a belt between 10 and 50 miles in width and about 200 miles in length. Seventeen million years ago magma began to rise beneath a Mount Emmons that hadn't yet formed. Steam in the magma bore a load of minerals in solution and sought its escape through the proliferation of cracks in the crust. The water never found the surface, and its load of minerals cooled and hardened into deposits. The molybdenum deposit beneath Mount Emmons takes the shape of a brain, an inverted bowl topping a pillar-like backbone of ossified magma. Mount Emmons itself was formed ten million years ago. Rising like a great pair of headless shoulders behind the town of Crested Butte, it lost its crest to glaciers. Now they call it the Red Lady, for its sunset glow.

AMAX refuses to divulge its reasons for choosing Mount Emmons for exploration, not wanting to give away the secret to the dozens of other mineral-exploration outfits now combing the national forest for likely looking outcrops. It is probable that the spot looked appealing for a couple of reasons. First, the exploration site was accessible by road, located as it is beneath the old Keystone mine. If a tree fell at Keystone, it would fall on AMAX. The Forest Service requires that drill rigs be helicoptered to roadless areas, having learned through experience that mining companies cut switchbacks on high-country tundra and that the roads become too eroded for revegetation—time passes slowly in the high country. Second, all AMAX had to do to get a good look at what was under Mount Emmons was look at the Keystone waste-rock pile.

Finding the mineral belt in the first place was not difficult. Two dozen other mining companies have found Gunnison County as well, and have made over 1,700 mining claims there. Molybdenum sulphide at Mount Emmons appears as dark gray bands in hunks of lighter gray hornfels. The rock is so highly fractured that there is not a cubic inch that doesn't remember when the magma came. The waste rock gave geologists their first clue, their drilling finds encouraged them, but when it was confirmed that their discovery was the fourth largest deposit of moly in the world at that time, the geologists literally did handsprings around the old Keystone. The confirmed deposit contains 155 million tons of ore. Each ton of ore contains eight pounds of moly. The market price of molybdenum at the time was $9.30 a pound. In return for a mineral deposit valued in the billions of dollars, AMAX would pay the Forest Service $5 an acre.

AMAX was the biggest mining company in the U.S., and number 55 on the *Fortune* 500 list. In 1979 its assets were $4 billion and its earnings $365 million. It produced half the molybdenum mined in the Western world. The two largest moly mines in the world were AMAX mines, right there in Colorado: the Climax and the Henderson mines.

Climax opened as a strip mine on Bartlett Mountain in 1918 and produced molybdenum unenthusiastically until 1929, when a Climax scientist finally conjured up some industrial uses for the stuff. If you look to the left as you go north on Highway 91 now, you won't find Bartlett Mountain at all; it can now be found on the right of the highway, ground to fine sand and spread over several square miles of valley floor as tailing. The rocks in Ten Mile Creek, leading away from the site, are orange; like Coal Creek, Ten Mile Creek has carried the acid outflow of the mine. Even AMAX executives agree that the site is a gaping nightmare—which they intend to clean up as best they can as soon as they've gotten the rest of the moly out.

The public outcry over the Climax ordeal made AMAX sensitive, and when the Henderson ore body was discovered beneath Red Mountain in 1967 the corporation tried to atone with its famous experiment in ecology. AMAX asked Dr. Betty Willard, a professor of high-altitude ecology at the University of Colorado and president of the Colorado Open Space Council (an association of environmentalist groups), to help plan its half-billion-dollar mine. Willard had previously been on President Johnson's Council for Environmental Quality before she became head of the Department of Engineering Ecology and Environmental Sciences at the Colorado School of Mines in Golden.

"At this point there were no environmental laws pushing this idea, just good judgment and forward thinking," Willard remembers. "You can't understand what AMAX is about until you see what they were able to do at Henderson. The young attorney who had been put in charge of making the initial investigation at Henderson thought, Gee, we ought to be able to do the Henderson mine better than we did Climax. The AMAX people talked it over and formed a communication design committee that met for eight years in designing that mine: myself, an attorney and planner, a metallurgist, a chemist, and a wilderness buff. We would sit down and meet with the top management of the mine. We got right in on the ground floor. We had a rule that anything and everything could be asked."

The Henderson ore body lies 4,000 feet beneath Red Mountain, right on the continental divide a few miles north of Loveland Pass and I-70. It contained enough ore to keep miners blasting 30,000 tons of ore a day for thirty years. As a miner from Silverton told Don Bachman, "That's not mining; that's underground construction." Red Mountain became an anthill for front-end loaders: AMAX dug fifty miles of tunnels in the mountain before starting up production. Henderson's mineshaft is the biggest in the world, a giant elevator lifting and hauling 230 miners at a scoop. The main technique used is block caving, the twentieth-century alternative to pick-and-shoveling—a section of mountain is undercut and blasted until all the rock falls down. "Utilizing the fractures that are natural in the rock," Dr. Willard explains, "you cause the ore body to come to you." The Henderson mine site takes up two square miles. The nearest town is twenty miles down the road.

The first thing Willard asked AMAX was, Why do mines always have to be so ugly? AMAX came back with light green aluminum siding and plans for a mineshaft whose large above-ground snout is made of natural rock. Willard was encouraged. The second thing she asked was, What are you going to do with your tailings?

"Of course, one of the biggest problems with any mining is tailings. Where are you going to put all that junk? With molybdenum, out of every ton of ore you only get a maximum of eight pounds of usable concentrate. The ore body was in Clear Creek, forty miles upstream from Denver in Denver's watershed. They told us, There is no place where we can think of putting a tailing pond on the east side of the divide. So we're going to put it on the other side of the divide.

"Well, we just fainted. They were going to go out about fifteen miles from the mine and have the mill clear on the other side of the divide. We couldn't believe our ears. First they thought they were going to pump the tailing over the hill, and the next thing we knew they were planning a railroad going out through the continental divide and emerging in the Williams Fork Valley, where they found a good site, and that's where it is now."

The Henderson mine went into production in 1976. A 9.6-mile railroad tunnel beneath the continental divide brings the ore to the mill. The broad valley above a small tributary of the Williams Fork is filling with the grit of 40 percent ground granite, mixed with 60 percent water, oil, and chemical-processing residue. Pumps run night and day, noisily, sucking out the water that seeps from the low dam that holds the tailing and sending it back to the mill for reuse. Some spills in the Williams Fork have been reported. A family of ducks has made its home in a pond of crusty water below the dam, and AMAX has sent biologists down to monitor their health. Above the tailing a flowering meadow and the elderly remains of a homesteader's cabin wait to be buried.

AMAX took infinite pains with the Henderson mine. A special little tunnel was built beneath the ore transport railway so that elk could migrate without being run over. Alpine tundra was taken up in large pieces and replanted after construction. Henderson requires tremendous amounts of electricity—it is Colorado's single largest energy user. AMAX brought the pylons of its power corridor in by helicopter and painted the 115-kilovolt towers a nice ecological green.

"We worked together as a group, a team, for eight years, working out every single consideration," Willard said. "I think today there is no better example in the world of how to do something big and industrial in the natural environment." In fact, the plan worked so well that AMAX wanted to reapply it at Mount Emmons.

* * * * *

"I don't care if they put colored balloons around the mill and paint the trucks to look like chipmunks," the town planner back in Crested Butte was telling the *Chronicle*. "We could possibly help them hide the impact and then everyone will think they're doing a good job. But there is no mistaking. The impact will be immense."

AMAX expected to bring a construction force of 1,000 workers and a mining force of 1,500 to the new mine. This 2,500, plus their families, would add 7,000 souls to a valley where 12,000 lived—the equivalent of twenty new people a day for a year. A population growth of over 10 percent a year for two or more years makes a boom, and a boomtown is no place to live.

When the Missouri Basin Power Project came to Wheatland, Wyoming, the town boomed. Wheatland Police Chief Evans reports, "Back when I started, I knew 90 percent of the people in town. Today I walk down the street and I don't recognize but four or five people. The department has grown from one squad car to four. In 1977, $15,000 worth of property was reported stolen. In 1979, in one month, stolen property was valued at $18,000. We never had any prostitution at all before the plant came. The bars fill up at eight o'clock in the morning, if they're not working at the plant. One night we had a hundred people fighting in one bar. In the years before the plant, rape was something that happened in the big cities, but never in Wheatland. Now we've been averaging three to four rape cases a year and a lot of others never get reported." In 1978 a group from Gunnison County toured a few boomtowns to try to grasp what they would be facing. They went to Gilette, Wheatland, and Wright City, Wyoming, and Craig, Colorado. They came back reporting "sheer terror."

Crested Butte's leadership went into shock. There was talk of cooperation and mitigation, and solace was found in the fact that AMAX was a good mining company to have for a neighbor, if you had to have a mining company for a neighbor. After a month or so the initial shock wore off. The town saw the bulldozer at the door, and the bulldozer did not look like a chipmunk.

"The immediate reaction was resignation. When the mine announced its plans, a lot of us wished they'd go away, and felt if we clapped our hands and prayed real hard they would have. But they didn't," says Don Bachman. "I don't know if I had very much to do with it, but I wrote a long letter to the *Crested Butte Chronicle* outlining a scenario of what I felt would occur if the mine came in. That turned out to be more of a self-fulfilling prophecy than I thought it was going to be."

Among Bachman's predictions: "The first development would be the upgrading of Highway 135 from Gunnison to Crested Butte. ... It is conceivable that the entire route could be four-laned."

AMAX did plan to improve that highway. The old road is dangerous, possibly fatal to the three shifts per day of miners who would be driving back and forth to town. But a new one would dominate the valley and put an end to Crested Butte's artful isolation.

Another part of Bachman's scenario was, "We could see utilities coming in from any direction including through what might be part of a proposed roadless area." AMAX planned two sets of power lines, and one corridor would run to the west, adjacent to a proposed wilderness area, to tap the electricity produced by a new coal-fired power plant. "It seems logical that production portals will be established at one or more of the Keystone levels. There could ... be major impact to the hydrologic ecology of the town's watershed when major construction and road building, additional housing, maybe a mill operation and extensive underground mining are all taking place in a very small area." The town has since passed an ordinance requiring that developers in the town's watershed obtain a permit. AMAX did not apply; instead, AMAX sued the town.

Bachman's easiest guess was, "A 400-person development crew moved in the next year and a 1,200-person production crew working twenty-four hours a day every day of the year for the next thirty-five years would sure add up to a nice busy little town here in the mountains." He concluded with a rallying toot: "Mount an intelligent and united force of opposition. Respect the AMAX people. Remember that they are every bit as dedicated to saving the environment and making a living as you are, they just have to mine the area first."

After six years of fighting development introduced by outsiders and prodevelopment interests within the county, Crested Butte's colonels had no problem mobilizing for their next skirmish. In the fall Mitchell was elected mayor on an anti-mine platform. He won by sixteen votes. A citizens' group, the High Country Citizens Alliance, was formed to garner grant money and collect contributions to fight the mine. The alliance immediately started working on designation of large portions of the West Elk Mountains as wilderness areas under the 1964 Wilderness Act. Mayor Mitchell began to use his own unusual person to attract media attention.

Mitchell is, by his own admission, a sideshow: "I love it. I'm a ham anyway." He lost his fingers and the essential outside layers of his face in 1972, when his motorcycle ran into a laundry truck in San Francisco and burst into flames. Doctors reconstructed him as best they could, and when his burns were healed Mitchell took himself and the proceeds from his lawsuit to Colorado. He decided to be a ski bum and landed in Crested Butte. A few years later Mitchell tried a take-off with ice on the wings of his newly purchased plane. The plane crashed and he became a paraplegic. While he was in the hospital his house caught fire. A sympathetic town rebuilt Mitchell's home, and it was ready by the time he left the hospital in a wheelchair. He showed his thanks by working sixty-hour weeks at a salary, designated by the town charter, of $25 per month. Mitchell had worked in radio before his accidents, and he thinks his voice saved him. "There's this burnt-up funny-looking guy with stubby fingers in a wheelchair, and he rolls up and you wonder if he can speak, and out flows a fairly well-modulated, sometimes articulate voice that tells you to get off your ass and do something." His voice fades: "I didn't consciously arrange it this way."

Mitchell is also a skillful politician. Just as Tommy Glass preached destiny, Mitchell preached values. "Today the very values which make our part of the Rockies so important are in conflict with the other values of great importance," he said during his traveling anti-AMAX slide show. "Coal, oil, shale, uranium, molybdenum, and once again silver and gold are sought after by a dizzying array of companies. In the coming years the decision-making process is going to determine the key question: Will Colorado become the world's newest Third World nation?

"Recreation is one of the reasons we have no unemployment in Gunnison County. We're told about the jobs that are going to be brought in because of mining. When you realize that Leadville (that's an AMAX company town) has one of the highest unemployment rates in Colorado, you realize that the mine is not going to create jobs. It's going to create unemployment.

"They tell me that molybdenum is an energy-saving material. It makes steel more weldable. AMAX announced not too long ago that the equivalent of the entire production of the Climax mine for two years, the largest moly mine in the world, will be used just to build the Alaskan gas pipeline. So we're going to tear down a mountain of coal to get the energy that will be needed to tear down a mountain of molybdenum, next to my home, to supply the moly to build the Alaskan gas pipeline, which will then supply the energy that we wasted tearing down the mountain of coal, tearing down the mountain of molybdenum, and building the gas pipeline.

"In Crested Butte, we have looked at the proposal to turn our low-crime, low-social problem, and highly productive community into another addition to AMAX's profit column. What we see is a huge public loss if such a project were to go ahead. It is the right of a small town to protect its own backyard and at the same time look beyond its borders to weigh the real costs and the net energy effect of such a proposal."

While Mitchell was out stumping, Crested Butte was simmering. AMAX was making plans to drive its first large tunnel into Mount Emmons. Someone took a shotgun to the window of the AMAX storefront. Children of AMAX executives ran home in tears, while the town's children taunted, "We made an AMAX girl cry." The Forest Service smelled sulphur. Owing to the apparent unrest in Crested Butte, the Forest Service halted development of the Mount Emmons tunnel until the Environmental Impact Statement (EIS) required by the National Environmental Protection Act of 1969 could be written and evaluated.

Some work at the Mount Emmons minesite had already proceeded as the EIS was being prepared. Administrative buildings were going up, roads were being cut, and AMAX had spent $18 million to clean up the Keystone drainage and tailing ponds that ruined Coal Creek so that fish could live there again. What wasn't tended was the high-altitude forest.

In the dry fall of 1979 a contractor working at the forested AMAX exploration site on Mount Emmons allowed some stray sparks to fall from a blowtorch. Smoke poured into the air and drifted toward Crested Butte. Don Bachman was one of the first arrivals from town—he had fought many fires, and the smoke had scared him. "AMAX tried to fight it themselves," Bachman remembers. "You have to realize it was highly visible from the town, really a fast-moving fire that was putting out a lot of smoke. When I got there it was pretty well out of control, and they had no fire-control plans. They were making a lot of efforts to get their drill rig out from the path of the fire rather than fighting the fire. I attempted to organize crews to go in with bulldozers, but the lack of organization on their part made our efforts pretty futile. In the end they had to build a giant fire line across the mountain and probably lost another ten to twenty acres." The fire burned for weeks in the duff. Fifty-five acres were lost, and when AMAX sent crews up to revegetate the site, the ground hadn't yet cooled. All the little seeds they sowed popped like popcorn.

* * * * *

Crested Butte's dislike of AMAX was reciprocated by the AMAX miners. "I think Crested Butte is a tragedy. It's people against technology. Technology never hurt anyone till some person misused it," said one. "The people in Crested Butte don't want the mine because they want to hang on to their drug culture," said another. "What right have they to keep the mine out? To me, miners are better educated and better traveled than any other group of people. That Mitchell thinks miners are riff-raff. That isn't so," said a third.

AMAX representative Joe Blumberg, an eight-year resident of Crested Butte who had been teacher and marshall in the town and who was happy to land one of the few high-paying white-collar jobs around, moved himself and his family to Gunnison. The town was giving him, as he said, bad vibes.

By this time most of the basement of the Forest Service's Gunnison office was given over to preparations for the EIS on the AMAX project. It was a room full of charts and maps and men dressed in Smoky Bear buff. They pondered the incalculable, going cross-eyed trying to enumerate the thumping changes mining would bring to the valley. They were open to suggestions.

Mitchell suggested to the Forest Service that they look more closely at the likelihood that Mount Emmons would cave in as it was mined. Mitchell's eyes, all that's left of the face he was born with, are blue, and they look gleeful when he describes AMAX's monumental slip-up at Henderson. One October the roof fell in over a portion of the Henderson mine excavation. This is called subsidence. No one was hurt, and the miners inside didn't even notice; it was reported by a miner on lunch break who saw it from across the valley. Before the cave-in, Red Mountain looked like a regular mountain. Now a sharply defined cork has been pulled from it. Were Red Mountain the size of an apple, the hole would be a toothy bite. "A couple of years ago they took me on a tour of the Henderson mine," Mitchell said. "They assured me there would be no subsidence at the Henderson mine at all, because they're digging 3,500 feet below the surface. A giant chunk of mountain caved over them after they'd only been mining for two years. No subsidence is in their operating plan for Mount Emmons. When they assure me their 155 million tons is only going to cause a little bit of damage, maybe in thirty years, I tend to be a little suspicious."

A glory hole changes the geomorphology of a mountain—it will outlast a mine by hundreds of thousands of years. Tailings outlast the mine as well, and the long-term effects of tailings were the most difficult to assess of AMAX's operations. Over a period of thirty years the ore inside Mount Emmons was to be hauled out, ground up, and beached in a valley near the mine. All AMAX needed was a broad valley of over 5,000 acres with a minimum of fetch (drainage area) in close proximity to the mine. AMAX chose a place called Alkali Basin.

Alkali Basin is a depression that hangs between Flat Top and Red mountains, overlooking Highway 135. When water runs off Flat Top into Alkali Creek it flows straight downhill to the East River and the Roaring Judy Fish Hatchery, where the state of Colorado grows trout fingerlings. Any accidental spillage from the tailing pond, any at all, would be sure to wipe out the fish hatchery with great speed. AMAX said that there wouldn't be an accident, for they would build a strong earth-filled dam to hold the tailings back (most tailing dams are made of the silty tailing). Trees would be planted on the dam to bar it from sight of the highway. The mine would tend the dam until the ore was gone, possibly until the year 2020. After that and for the rest of geological time the untended tailing would overhang the river.

Alkali Basin is a misnomer. It is a bowl of sage ringed by aspen, with a broad sunny south-facing slope. It contains one of the largest tribes of sage grouse in Colorado; the basin is their booming grounds. In the spring the grouse get out on their booming grounds and make calls you can hear for half a mile. They obviously enjoy it; they do it for almost two months, starting when the snow begins to melt and carrying on until May.

Alkali Basin is also a place where elk calve, migrate, and find forage in winter. When the snow gets deep in Gunnison County the elk huddle down into the valleys. Only 11 percent of the county is available to animals in winter. Of that, only half is public land. According to the game wardens, one of the largest and healthiest elk populations in the state uses the area as winter range. There was a time when, as one valley with a broad and sunny slope was developed, the elk could find another valley to graze on in winter. The game warden's concern about losing Alkali Basin was a matter of totting up the valleys remaining and finding that the elk had probably just about run out of choices.

* * * * *

Starting in 1979 and continuing throughout the next three years, the Forest Service collected information for its EIS. This included the concerns (in writing) of the affected community groups and the documents submitted by the various government agencies responsible for the land, air, and water of the valley, as well as AMAX's proposed operating plans. The purpose of the EIS was neither to lead the Forest Service to approve nor disapprove the project as such, but instead to allow it to assess the environmental impacts of the plan overall and in all its detail. Then the Forest Service would be able to recommend action on the basis of comparisons between competing alternative plans. If the environmental effects of a proposal could not be mitigated the Forest Service would recommend an alternative.

Such careful and open examination would seem likely to encourage discussion and thus understanding among the groups involved. On the Mount Emmons project, however, positions were fully entrenched before the EIS was begun, and as the assessment process moved forward the combatants settled in for a long stand-off.

Mayor Mitchell, a deft media manipulator, made the general public an ally by coaxing national television and magazine reporters to paint Crested Butte as a gallant David battling the Goliath-like AMAX. For a brief time Crested Butte's plight enjoyed star billing and the fleeting sympathy of the ever-distractable public at large. Locally, however, feelings ran deeper and sympathy was less easily generated. The Crested Butte anti-mine activists alienated not only the AMAX management and a few of the old-timers, but also quite a few of the small-towners who lived twenty-eight miles down the valley in Gunnison, where the mountains flattened out to become high sage desert.

In his many public appearances Mitchell spoke passionately about preserving a wide area around Crested Butte that he called "Gunnison country"—the large, varied, and spectacularly beautiful stretch of eagle's-nest mountains and jack-rabbit desert of which Crested Butte, snuggled up in the valley, was but a small part. In Gunnison, the county seat, with a population of about six thousand, not everyone appreciated Mitchell's protection. By and large, Gunnison's retailers, its small business people, and its agribusiness people had lived and worked in Gunnison all the while Crested Butte was winking in and out of boom and bust, and had been there for many years before Mitchell ever visited Colorado. Given a choice between cozying up behind Crested Butte and playing ball with AMAX, Gunnison's leaders chose to play ball.

Basically, their fixes on the situation were different. In Crested Butte, the dreaded possibility of wide highways full of traffic, huge power lines, disturbed wildlife, and all the physical mayhem of industry brought the townspeople's environmental concerns to the fore. Gunnison, on the other hand, was where the 1,400 workers would actually live. New housing in the Crested Butte area was not going up with miners' bankrolls in mind, consisting as it did of a large selection of $100,000 condos; the construction and mining people, all parties agreed, would live in Gunnison. So, aided in part by grants from AMAX, Gunnison's municipal government prepared for the onslaught by expanding their school capacity, social services, and sewage plant. They increased the wages and size of the police force, and added staff planners, engineers, and a computer at City Hall. AMAX subdivided a meadow near Gunnison and began to build eight hundred new homes.

A similar, cooperative program to mitigate disruption was not accomplished by AMAX and the Crested Butte town council, since diplomatic relations between the town and company had long since ceased. "That mine won't be built," Mitchell kept asserting. "We decided on that." And he was right: the town had decided just that, in a resolution passed unanimously by the council in 1979.

By 1981, Gunnison was gearing up to meet the future, while Crested Butte's bulwarks were beginning to crumble. Many placed much hope in the legal strategies of Wes Light, the attorney for the High Country Citizens' Alliance, who seized every opportunity to block AMAX. One long shot had been to call into play a law originally designed to allow small towns to protect clean-water sources. Under this law, Crested Butte's town council passed a municipal water ordinance, ostensibly to protect Coal Creek upstream, above the Keystone tailing site, where water from the creek flowed into the town's cistern. In effect, the town sought to commandeer one side of Mount Emmons. With ordinance in hand, Crested sued the company; the outcome, however, proved disappointing. AMAX lawyers contended that the town's municipal authority did not extend into the many acres that made up Coal Creek's watershed, and the High Country Citizens' Alliance was unable to prove otherwise.

A second defensive measure was to petition the Forest Service to recommend to Congress that Oh Be Joyful Creek and its attendant watershed be designated a wilderness area. Oh Be Joyful Creek was flanked by two existing wilderness areas, Raggeds and West Elk, and its location upside of Mount Emmons would have inhibited AMAX expansion there. The Forest Service refused the petition, and Crested Butte tried another gambit. The odds on this last effort's succeeding were perhaps poorest of all.

Crested Butte's anti-mine group tried to squash the mine project simply by using its right to raise issues of concern for Forest Service examination in the EIS process. The group was game to try anything legal, however, so many of the issues they raised attacked the notion that the loss they faced could be mitigated. One question the town offered to the Forest Service for consideration read: "How can a small town control its destiny when faced with a large mineral development operating under the 1872 Mining Law?" Next question: "Does AMAX have the right to use U.S. Forest Service lands for their profit-making venture, while disturbing the fragile balance between ecological tranquillity and the successful tourist-based economy the town has strived so hard to achieve?" And: "How do you weigh the values of small-town living, the psychic benefits of trusting neighbors and slow pace, against the value of molybdenum?" These were not the kinds of issues that the lawmakers who had established the National Environmental Protection Act (NEPA) had envisioned.

"The question of whether the public interest is being served by the use of this land isn't one that the Forest Service has ever discussed," Mitchell explained. "NEPA requires the Forest Service to look at a bunch of alternatives. One alternative is to take the proponent's proposal and then say, 'Go ahead,' and let them run the bulldozer. Another alternative is to say, 'Let's mitigate.' The third alternative, one the Forest Service has never considered before, is no action. We for the first time are getting the Forest Service at least to acknowledge that the no action alternative exists."

While they weighed these and other questions in the EIS, the Forest Service's researchers wore what District Ranger Mike Curran called "NEPA hats," and NEPA took precedence. When the EIS was completed, however, out would come the 1872 Mining Law hats, which would give the Forest Service no choice but to approve the mine.

Federal machinery grinds slowly. According to Don Bachman, however, this coincided with Crested Butte's strategy. For, as he explained, dawdling and delaying allowed Crested Butte to take advantage of one important factor that AMAX could not control: the state of the molybdenum market. Insisting that AMAX follow the letter of the law in all its ponderous detail was one way to buy time and thus keep AMAX's investment in the project to a minimum. By 1981, total investment was about $150 million. Had the project proceeded as AMAX engineers had originally scheduled it, tens of millions of dollars more would have been spent and actual construction of the shafts would have been begun more than two years before.

Crested Butte's strategists' theory was that AMAX was more likely to bow out of a planned mine than an actual one. "I don't think anyone in the boardroom is going to blink an eye if they decide to pull out on that investment," said Bachman, whose truck sported a bumper sticker proclaiming "Not a ton in '81."

In the end, Bachman's bumper sticker proved prophetic. By August 1981 several huge new moly mines had come on line in the United States, and at the same time alloy-steel production was dropping. The price of moly had fallen to around $6 a pound. AMAX was stockpiling the output of its two Colorado mines, equipment was standing idle at Climax, and at both mines layoffs were expected. Thus, it was not the fact of the announcement so much as its timing that surprised the Crested Butte people when, in August 1981, half way through a regular meeting of the Gunnison County Planning Commission, AMAX announced that construction on the Mount Emmons mine would be delayed until at least 1984. The Crested Butte contingent was ecstatic, and everyone, Gunnison businessmen and old-timers alike, admitted to a long sigh of relief. When the EIS approving the mine came out the following year, it was anticlimactic.

* * * * *

Today, AMAX's claim on Mount Emmons stands idle. The company's fortunes changed the year it left Crested Butte. Nineteen eighty-four came and went, the mine went from "delayed" through "back-burnered" to "for sale." From the offers it's been getting, AMAX doesn't expect to recoup its $150 million investment.

Since 1981 the price of moly has continued to drop. By the end of 1982, the Climax mine had shut down entirely, and the Henderson soon followed suit. Both mines are now producing again, but their output is low. The price of moly has dropped to between $3.00 and $3.50 a pound. The metals market in general hasn't been kind to companies like AMAX; in these bust years company people are pleased enough when the company breaks even.

Below the mountain, though, Crested Butte has changed. Residents lock their doors at night. The streets have been paved. The ski area has grown, although bad weather still thwarts regular winter shuttle flights from Denver. The meadows where cattle used to graze are full of new buildings. Anyone who asks for a home on the range can have it now in Crested Butte, and if he wants a sauna or a Jacuzzi he can have that, too. It's just not the same old place anymore.

Not long after AMAX announced its change of plans, Mitchell ran for a third term as mayor. He was defeated, 313 votes to 247, by Tom Cox, half of the Elk Avenue real estate firm of Cox and Hagen. Cox ran on a pro-development platform. According to the *Crested Butte Chronicle,* Mitchell had "lost touch with his constituency." The new administration was backed by a pro-growth crowd, the newest newcomers, who wanted to mend fences both with Gunnison and the ski industry. These were people in their twenties and thirties who saw Crested Butte as "a place of opportunity, rather than a counter-culture environment," according to City Councilman Gary Sporcich, son of an old-time miner.

Not long after the election, Mitchell fell in love and got married, to the delight and surprise of his many friends in town, as well as his own. He has expanded his horizons politically; though he lost a bid for the U.S. House of Representatives in 1984, he planned to run for Lieutenant Governor in 1986.

Back when AMAX announced that the mine had been delayed, Crested Butte waxed joyful. A television-news helicopter airlifted Mitchell to the top of Mount Emmons, where credit for the successful rout of AMAX was duly doled out.

"It's easy for the activists to claim victory," said an AMAX spokesman, "but it was really the economy that got us."

The people of Crested Butte had been there before: boom and bust is the history of their town, and most probably its future as well. The world's third largest molybdenum deposit rests beneath Mount Emmons, and they don't believe it will be allowed to stay hidden there forever.

CHAPTER THREE

The Gold of the Gurglers

THE Austrian village of Obergurgl, 6,330 feet up in the Austrian Alps just north of the Italian border, is closer to God than most places. The highest parish in Europe, it lies in the pebbled lap of the Gurgler glacier—named for the sound its meltwater makes as it flows down the long and narrow Oetztal.

On the turnabout beside the church, in a house his family has occupied since the thirteenth century, lives Martin Scheiber Broser. With his green Tyrolean hat, his curved pipe dangling from his mouth, and his blue workman's smock, Broser is a postcard Tyrolean. And the image goes beneath the surface, too: along with only five or six Gurgler farmers—he still carries on a tradition that began a thousand years ago. In the spring he drives his sheep over the glaciers and out of Obergurgl's valley to the high pastures on the other side of the mountain; in the fall he drives them back to the southern side of the Alps. The border imposed by the Treaty of St. Germain, which in 1919 divided the Tyrol in two, never stopped the farmers—the sheep had to eat.

On any given morning, Broser can be found passing over the lane behind his 800-year-old house to his 200-year-old barn—the majority of Obergurgl's buildings date from the years since 1965—to look after his cows, goats, and sheep. His fields of grass and his animals are his pride. In times past, his ancestors had proudly dubbed their meadows the "gold of the Gurglers."

This gold is hard to mine. In April, when the pastures of the lower Oetztal are springing green, the Gurglers are often still up to their ears in snow. With the snow still thick on the ground in June, Obergurgl's farmers have sometimes had to drag manure to the fields on snowsledges. When the snow melts, Broser has to maintain stone-lined irrigation ditches high across the rough and steep mountainside in order to water the scattered patches of grass that yield his hay crop. What the Gurglers' animals produced—meat, wool, and cheese—has never been enough, and a century ago the Gurglers suffered from chronic malnutrition. In fact, hunger, or fear of it, sometimes pushed the Gurglers to drastic extremes. To curb their numbers, for example, the villagers once agreed to ban new marriages. In a devout community, this was a sure way to control the growth of the population, and between July 7, 1831, and April 8, 1850, there was not one wedding. The story is that only one couple produced an illegitimate child. They left town, as did 121 other people. The ban proved an effective means of birth control: a hundred years ago there were only about a hundred people in the village.

Today, neither Broser's family nor the other farming families in Obergurgl depends solely on its animals for its living. The food the farmers produce goes to the restaurants, and in the last couple of decades the Brosers have established a phonebook's worth of other businesses: a taxi company (Broser and his sons are the drivers), a guest house, the only motel-style apartment complex in town, a sausage and spirits shop, a currency exchange, and a travel agency. The Brosers' diversification reveals a fundamental change—tourists are the new harvest of Obergurgl.

* * * * *

The big Hotel Edelweiss towers above the church spire. Balconies jut from the hotel's walls like sprockets from a gear. The

Oetztaler Express bus from Innsbruck rolls in like clockwork every two hours, picking up and dropping off skiers. The village is as crowded as an amusement park. The eastern side of the valley hums with the cables of twenty-one chair lifts. Over the slopes the snowcats comb the snow and rumble. Along the village's only street the seventy hotels, pensions, and guest houses cluster like sheep in a snowstorm. At night the village is a yellow beacon in a dark mountain wasteland, a place where beer-sodden skiers can lurch home in three-quarter time, safe from the unfriendly mountains, with an oom-pah-pah back beat to guide them. The skiers are content: they have found what they seek in Obergurgl. They return there winter after winter, and they keep the Gurglers prosperous.

It's a stuffy little valley, encircled by ridges. To the west is Broser's nearly vertical pasture; to the east, the ski slopes. The Gurgler glacier protects the south, and in the north, blocking the view down the river, is the Oxenkopf, an excrescence of rock whose shape resembles the head of an ox. Obergurgl's hotels clump at the bottom of the isolated valley like marbles in a bowl, so deeply you can't see the high peaks from their windows. The best view is from the Hotel Gotthard, built in 1965 and owned by Gotthard Scheiber (a cousin of Martin Broser's, though neither man pursues the connection with any enthusiasm), who is president of the village tourist board and second son of the richest family in Obergurgl. Now in his early forties, though he looks younger, Scheiber is a tall man with a high forehead, round blue eyes, and hair clipped short. A slight case of polio when he was small has left him with a dragging leg, but he is far from handicapped. He is a good skier. As with many of the Gurglers these days, his ski goggles have left his face with a banded tan; he looks like a raccoon in negative.

The Scheibers are an enterprising family. The eldest brother owns two hotels; the youngest has built his own ski village, Hochgurgl, high on a mountain sheep pasture along the road to the border. Their good fortune came from their grandfather, Martinus Scheiber, who was the village's first hotelier. A life-sized bronze statue of Martinus now stands before the church, his gleaming beard curling youthfully and a climbing rope slung over one shoulder. The big tourist buses that come from Innsbruck take their U-turns around him as his lifted arm points forever toward the mountains. It is a proud family.

A hundred years ago Martinus Scheiber became Obergurgl's original tourism booster. He sponsored the construction of the first Alpine huts in the Oetztaler Alps—warm, beery ports where hikers could lodge for the night. In 1887 he built the Edelweiss, Obergurgl's first hotel, which today towers over the church. His was the first telephone in the village; its wires followed the cowpath from the village of Sölden, nine miles down the valley. Because one in five tourists was from England, he encouraged his daughter to learn English; she was the first in the village to do so.

The English people Martinus Scheiber's daughter spoke to were brave pioneers in what was then considered to be a death-defying sport. Until about halfway through the nineteenth century, mountains were considered by many Englishmen and other Europeans to be dangerous, dragon-filled places. When railroads brought the Alps a little closer to the cities, however, explorers brought back more reassuring reports. In 1870 Edward Whymper, the famous scrambler up the Matterhorn, reported (only half jokingly) that attaining the heights did not make him throw up, that the sky viewed from the peaks did not appear to be black, and that at mountaintop he was not afflicted with a wild desire to toss himself off the edge. Mountaineering soon became the rage of the upper classes.

Whymper himself journeyed to the Oetztal and recorded his visit in paintings. There were other visitors, too. The village priest's diary of 1864 recounts the visit of a German professor and his wife. The priest led the couple to the glacier where, to his puzzlement, the woman removed her clothing and proceeded to do calisthenics in a crevasse. Countless others came as well. For a while the priest, whose home was the only lodging for the public, was stocking them two to a bed. The usually stolid Oetztalers were amazed. "If the visitors had to work here for only three weeks," wrote one Oetztaler near the end of the century, "they would lose their delight in the mountain world and they, too, would say, 'You damned nature!' "

Martinus Scheiber's sons kept the lead in the village. Angelus was one of the first skiers in the valley. As his aged sister remembers, Angelus came across a tourist one January just after the turn of the century. He and some other boys noticed that the tourist was sliding down the mountain on boards seven-and-a-half feet long strapped to his feet. The boys decided that the tourist was crazy, but, as the old woman tells it, they were crazy too. They found some old slats in a barn and bound their stiff-soled work shoes to them with pegs. Like beginning skiers everywhere, they schussed on luck and tumbled to a stop. To gain altitude they tied skins to the skis and walked up the mountain. In 1916 Angelus learned a more sophisticated skiing technique as a skiing rifleman in the Italian Alps. He saw the opportunities in teaching the theory behind the glide, and upon his discharge he started Obergurgl's first ski school.

In the 1920s similar businesses appeared throughout the Tyrol, and Angelus found himself competing with all the other villages in the valley. A paved road was built out of Obergurgl—a necessity if this hard-to-reach village was to have the skiers' business. Advertisements were published that lied a bit when they guaranteed avalanche-free roads all the way up the valley (this guarantee has yet to be met). Guided ski tours were mapped out through the local mountains. But the Gurglers had more of a reputation for taciturnity and bad weather than for providing holiday pleasure. Then, in 1931, Professor Auguste

Piccard fell from the sky onto the Gurgler glacier, leaving Obergurgl with an appetite for business it has yet to satisfy.

Professor Piccard, a Swiss-born physicist from the University of Brussels, had gone up in a balloon in order to study cosmic rays without atmospheric interference. Piccard and his assistant, Claude Kipfer, rose into the air to great fanfare on May 25, 1931, from a spot in Augsburg, West Germany. He knew that breathing ten miles above the earth would be impossible, and so he had designed a gondola for his balloon, a spherical metal capsule that would maintain a secure atmospheric pressure. Piccard's plan was to ascend, measure atomic particles, and then descend to the place where he had begun. To his great chagrin it was quite windy up there, and Piccard and Kipfer's balloon was blown toward the Alps and lost from view. They were presumed dead and overnight became newsreel heroes. The entire Western world waited for word from them.

Two evenings later mysterious lights flashed over the Gurgler glacier. The next morning a shepherd noticed a bright yellow splash on the glacier. He told a mountain guide, and the guide told Hans Falkner (the local schoolmaster and Angelus Scheiber's brother-in-law). Falkner dismissed his students from school and he and the guide set off. By mid-afternoon they had reached the gondola. From the tracks in the snow they could tell that the battered gondola had bounced when it landed and rolled down the ice, dragging the exhausted balloon behind it. Falkner whistled and called, but heard no reply. Beside the gondola he found a bottle with a note inside announcing, "Je suis Piccard."

Below the balloon, lying on warm rocks, Falkner found Kipfer and Piccard. They had no idea where they were. Piccard tried several languages before finding one in which they could communicate. "You are in Austria," Falkner finally told them in German. Piccard said the release valve on the balloon had jammed. He had been unable to regulate his ascent, and the balloon had taken off like a rocket. For two days they had drifted out of control, prisoners of the air. Finally, in the cold air above the glaciers, Piccard was able to release the valve. They crash-landed. Piccard had stowed small pillow-filled baskets aboard the gondola, but the makeshift crash helmets hadn't worked well. The two men had bounced around in the cabin like dice in a cup, and Kipfer was woozy from concussion. Piccard's instruments were mangled.

While Falkner's partner stayed to help the men off the glacier, Falkner hurried back to Obergurgl with three telegram messages in his pocket: one for Piccard's wife, one for Kipfer's, and one for the king of Belgium, who had sponsored the trip.

It was as if the Wizard of Oz had appeared in person in Obergurgl to grant everyone his dearest wish. Within hours European newspapermen were packed off to the Alps. Piccard's rescue made headlines in New York, and Obergurgl became the new mecca for the trendy. At last the Gurglers had something unique to advertise. For a year the mountain guides, Hans Falkner and Angelus Scheiber among them, beat the glacial snow into hardpack guiding curiosity-seekers to the stalled gondola.

The gondola had lodged in an awkward spot, high on a steep slope above a pond of icy water dammed by the glacier's toe. Beneath the ice dam sank the rocky gorge of the Gurgl. To remove the gondola would require a team of skiers to drag the sphere back up the rise and around the gorge. A special sledge was designed and built by an Innsbruck blacksmith, but when he arrived in Obergurgl with his contraption none of the village men would help him tow. Possession of the gondola was good business, and no one wanted to relinquish the windfall prematurely.

With a crew from another village, the blacksmith again attempted a rescue. He directed that the gondola be first pulled uphill to a place where it could be removed more safely. It was a long day's work, and the crew retired for the night to the nearest

Alpine hut. But the next morning the returning crew couldn't spot the gondola. The tracks of Obergurgler feet surrounded the spot where it had rested; the gondola had been rolled into a crevasse and was stuck there as snug as a cork. The blacksmith blamed Angelus Scheiber for organizing the trick, but laying blame didn't help. Moving the gondola was beyond human strength, and there it stayed for another month until a team of horses and men from Innsbruck yanked it free and pulled it down in one long and closely monitored day.

* * * * *

Piccard's adventure had a lasting effect. Angelus Scheiber had recently built a hotel, the Gurgl, in an empty field that was unfortunately too close to the mountainslope and prone to avalanches. With the money he made from the new tourist influx he moved his hotel to a spot beside his father's Edelweiss; the two hotels are now joined. (A new hotel was recently built on the site of the old Gurgl, even though the location still isn't safe. In 1976 an avalanche ground to a halt just outside the windows of the new hotel's indoor swimming pool, to the terror of the bathers. Neither they nor the pool was touched, but four cars and the parking lot were buried beneath the mass.)

For Falkner, on the other hand, notoriety was but the stepping-stone to more business. With his good command of English he found an off-season job in London as the resident Austrian winter sports advisor in a large department store. He extolled the beauties of Obergurgl and acquired some wealthy enthusiasts who, for much of the 1930s, followed him back home to Obergurgl. For a while, and at least partly thanks to Adolf Hitler, the village entertained more British than German skiers. In the mid-1930s, Hitler had imposed a tax of one thousand marks on Germans visiting Austria, an action that dealt a severe blow to Austria's burgeoning ski industry, heavily dependent as it had been on German visitors. In London, Falkner had spoken freely against the Nazis, and when Germany annexed Austria in 1938 he was one of the first to be arrested by the new, pro-Nazi regime. A former skiing student of his who was also a Canadian government official quickly intervened. Within a week Falkner became an immigrant to Canada.

In Quebec Falkner learned the business of New World skiing. In the Laurentians he managed what was then the biggest ski resort in Canada. He bought a ranch in Ontario, forty times the size of Obergurgl's small valley. But Falkner found himself overwhelmed with the space. He missed his snug valley so much that in 1951 he went home.

Back in the mountains, hard times had set in. A few of Falkner's former pupils hadn't returned from the war. In 1945 not one single tourist had found his way to Obergurgl, the first time this had happened in almost a hundred years. Skiing was only just beginning to make a bashful comeback when Falkner arrived home, and the skiers were still climbing the hills with skins strapped to their skis, just as they had when Angelus was a child.

Falkner had acquired American notions and Canadian money, and he believed in machines. He purchased a chair lift for Obergurgl, which he erected directly in front of the patio door of Angelus Scheiber's Hotels Edelweiss and Gurgl. The pieces of mountain meadow beneath the lift were leased from the farmers of Obergurgl (who hold the meadows as joint property), and a ski-lift company was formed to handle the business. It was the first of twenty-two ski lifts (the last was assembled in 1979) eventually operated under the aegis of that company, which Falkner still runs as president. Falkner, now in his seventies, still uses it nearly every day to ski in the winter. He lives beside the ski school in the only remaining private, not-open-for-guests house in all of Obergurgl.

Following Falkner's initial innovations, Obergurgl grew rapidly.

By 1969 engineers had netted the Alps thoroughly in superhighways, and the Gurglers were able to tap the main line of German tourist traffic directly. The village is only ninety minutes by road from Innsbruck, just over an hour from the rival ski resorts of the Arlberg, and less than half a day from Münich. The Gurglers welcomed the returning tourists like long-lost relatives, served them lowland German food in the restaurants, and abandoned their countrified Oetztaler dialect in favor of precise high German—all to please the guests.

There seemed an infinite supply of guests, so new hotels were built to house them and old guest houses were expanded. Even the priest owned a guest house, which he called, appropriately, Haus Kuraten. Nearly every lot had a hotel. By the time Gotthard Scheiber built his Hotel Gotthard, in 1965, there was not much land left; he chose one of the lots on top of the Kressbrunnen, the hill named for the spring-fed watercress that had once graced this cow pasture. The farmer who sold the Kressbrunnen had divided the land into small lots. Over a dozen hotels were erected there, and it wasn't long before the hoteliers began to argue among themselves over parking rights. The hill lost its watercress and gained a new name, Lawyers' Hill, in acknowledgment of the only people who were finally pleased by the situation.

The village began to seem like a life-sized Monopoly game. Nearly 40,000 tourists were spending 350,000 nights in Obergurgl's rented beds each year. From a parochial group of farmsteads Obergurgl had turned into an industrial town whose sole output was entertainment. Every person in town lived on the industry. But in the process of growth, Obergurgl never managed to acquire the corresponding salt of ordinary village life. There is no bakery, no shoe-repair shop, no hardware store, no greengrocer, no apothecary. Food is trucked in for the restaurateurs. Space had become too precious to spend on anything but tourists. For the raw materials of their success—dependable snow, green meadows, and sunsets that turned the peaks the colors of gold and blood—the Gurglers trusted providence. Here, mountains didn't mold lives anymore; with the machines that smooth the ski slopes of boulders and dips, the Gurglers molded the mountains. For the first time in the village's long history, Obergurgl's future seemed without limits.

* * * * *

In the summer of 1969, Obergurgl rang with hammer blows and the buzz of chain saws. Ten hotels were going up at once. That was the summer that Professor Walter Moser, a botanist from the University of Innsbruck, took over the administration of the university's *Alpine Forschungsstelle* (Alpine Research Station), which had been set up in the stone barracks that Hitler's troops had built at the edge of the village and abandoned after the war. For Moser the assignment was like a homecoming. He had been born and raised in nearby Langenfeld and had never strayed far from the valley. Of all the professors from the University of Innsbruck who could have taken on the research station and its studies in alpine ecology, Moser was the only Oetztaler. Though his childhood had been spent in a lower, softer part of the valley, he believed he understood the Gurglers, who had traditionally envied the lower Oetztalers for having an easier life. Once, when Moser returned to Obergurgl after spending three months in Edmonton, on the plains of Alberta, the Gurglers asked him how he liked it. "It's not like here," he replied. "It's wide open, and flat." "You must be used to that," one of the farmers rejoined. "You're from Langenfeld."

For two years before coming to Obergurgl Moser had conducted his studies atop the Nebelkogel, the foggy peak above the valley between Langenfeld and Obergurgl. The university owned a small research station at the 10,440-foot line there, perched on a rock ridge, lonely as a caboose on a trestle. In good weather it was a five-hour uphill trek to reach the shack, but in winter Moser sometimes had to climb for fourteen hours with the sounds of avalanches in his ears. The shack held a cot, scientific instruments, Moser, and nothing more. He worked alone, studying the primary production systems of tundra plants. His research was a contribution to UNESCO's International Biological Program, an idealistic program that sought to discover how much food the world could produce. It soon became obvious that in order to measure the output of human food it would be necessary to determine the production of bacterial, fungal, botanical, avian, reptilian, and mammalian food as well. The study became one that embraced ecosystems. Moser was looking for a way to approach the question, When is primary production stopped by nature? He hoped to find the answer on the Nebelkogel, above the stress zone that stops the growth of trees, above the zone where small shrubs give up and die, above the cutoff zone of the high grassland, amid the small cushion plants.

Moser, a tall, lanky man, is an accomplished musician. Before he left Langenfeld he had been leader of the village band. An evening walker near the Nebelkogel would often hear the sound of a violin singing one strand of a string quartet. Moser would be playing the other three parts in his mind, staving off the loneliness with his bow. The village was a pleasant change, then, and upon his arrival he strolled around the place striking up conversations with all who had time to stop. He asked to attend the annual meeting of the local tourist board, and found that the matter at hand was a discussion about building a new ski lift at the end of the valley. Moser was appalled. The villagers were about to bulldoze the forest to make yet another slope for skiers.

"If you go into the village," Moser remembers, "you see the hotels, then you see the forest. Then above these you see the glacier and the mountains, the ice-and-snow wall. It was striking: why had they never cut this forest? It was much more accessible than all the other wood below the village, but they never used it in the past. I don't know why even now. Maybe this was a simple reaction of these people, the last living barrier against the terrible ice."

The villagers' desire to cut down their forest, which they had always protected before, shocked him. "When the forest is protected not by law, but by tradition," he argues, "how could these people lose their feeling and respect for the landscape? But the Gurglers just laughed and said, 'What is the government to do if the next night the trees are cut? Who is to replace them? Of course we will be punished, but it is not a matter of money.' "

There were a couple of things at work in the Gurglers' decision. They had determined, and rightly, that they needed another kind of ski slope, and the topography and the avalanches were limiting their choice. The ski slopes of Obergurgl run to the high and steep pleats of the mountains. In poor weather, not uncommon in this valley, the slopes had to be closed for the safety of the skiers. The lower runs, more protected from the weather, were overloaded at these times. The villagers knew that to build another low-slope ski run would improve business in the village.

The other factor was political. Falkner, the Scheibers, and others had been leasing the land on which they built their lifts from the farmers who owned the land. There was constant rivalry in the village between what one farmer called the great families and the small families: the distinction is between the families that were successful in business and the families that entered the tourism business later and on a smaller scale. The farming families, which are considered small, owned the land. They kept guest houses and restaurants, and they kept pigs and sheep and cows, but they had not been the first to cash in on the tourist trade—the only lift owned by the farmers was on a beginner's slope; all the rest belonged to Falkner's company.

Home is a place the Gurgler farmers love to hate. Moser found that they wouldn't listen to outright pontification about the value of nature, although at first he tried. "Wait a minute," he told them. "What do you have for the summer tourist? You are always planning for the winter tourist, and all you will have for the summer people is warm soup three times a day and some fresh air. Is this enough for your guests? Don't you need this beautiful old forest?"

According to Moser, the villagers responded by saying, "We need the tourists. We need the slope. We need the money."

"And I said, 'It doesn't work that way,' " remembers Moser. "'Wait one season. Don't cut those trees this year, and I will provide an alternative.' "

Moser saw a time coming when the original gold of the Gurglers would be lost forever beneath the development of the ski industry. He was afraid that the summer hikers who still came to Obergurgl would soon no longer find there what they sought, and would choose less-developed valleys to visit. It was as if an old fairy tale were being enacted. For the valley, tourism was the goose that laid the golden egg, and now it seemed as if the villagers were about to strangle it. Moser decided to rescue the goose.

Moser did a very clever man, as Martin Broser likes to say. He called on the young schoolmaster and offered to teach the children for a day. The next day he showed up for class in his sturdy shoes and his gray Tyrolean jacket with buttons of polished antler. "Tell me all you know about this forest," he said. So all afternoon they talked about the birds and the squirrels, the stones and the trees, the rapids in the little gorge of the Gurgl River. The next day Moser led an expedition of thirty-seven children, ages six through ten, on the fifteen-minute walk to the forest. It was June and the sun was deliciously hot. They stopped beneath a tree, where Moser spoke of what he knew about the flowers and the plants, and the ethics of poking about in anthills. Then, because school was nearly over, he gave them an assignment for the summer. "Every time you come to this forest, pick something up, and in the fall you will write me a nice story about it," he said.

"In the summer I would come back from time to time," Moser recalls, "and this was my most exciting summer in Obergurgl. When I walked through the village with my university students, a door would open and a young child would come running out of the house, and he would cry 'Dr. Moser, Dr. Moser, I found this, and this.' And he would have stones in his pocket, and he would say, 'What a stone, it is so nice, I *found* it!' And I would step aside from my class and explain to him about the stone, and then I would discover his mother peeking through the door, and she was so proud. This I did to reactivate the people's emotions about the forest. They were still there, but they had been covered by the technology and the tourism business."

In the fall, as promised, the essays were written, and pictures drawn. The pictures were full of mountains, their silhouettes regularly serrated like sawblades. In the drawings people strolled in the forest, people with large hands, and Moser thinks this is the way the children saw the tourists: taking, always taking. "Did you ever hear anything about nature conservancy?" one essay asks. "Do not disturb the ants," says another, and, "It is a very nice forest, and an old one." A contest was arranged, and the winners received rucksacks—Broser's teenage daughters still use theirs—and Moser had the submissions compiled into a guidebook that forest walkers could buy as a souvenir. The forest is known as the Children's Forest now, and no one, says Moser, has again talked of cutting the trees.

After this incident Moser began to appear, like a noisy conscience, whenever the valley people opted for short-term gain over long-term preservation. It had become apparent that he and the people of Obergurgl had entirely different ideas over what pushed the valley to the limit. The townsfolk are by no means unintelligent. They're renowned throughout the valley for their hard-nosed business acumen. But their ideas and Moser's differed. Moser was concerned about the hidden price that might be extracted by the villagers' enthusiasms for business, but as far as the farming people were concerned the mountains still held the power in the valley. They believed that some redecoration in this little valley would make no difference to the storm of peaks that lifted permanently behind their horizon. They didn't realize that they were repeating the same pattern that had already occurred throughout mountainous Austria, a pattern that some referred to as the "Californiation" of the Alps.

* * * * *

The skiers and hikers who came were a demanding lot. They demanded comfort, but they also demanded that the mountains appear as pristine as they imagined mountains should be. If they didn't find both comfort and Alpine beauty in Obergurgl, they'd look elsewhere.

A comfortable domestic environment was well in hand. In Gotthard Scheiber's fine hotel, oriental rugs cushioned ski-booted feet. Outside the hotel the skiers seldom walked at all. They could zip from their bedsheets right onto the ski slopes, with barely a pause for door jambs. They took their coffee in silver pots and wiped their chins with fine linen.

But it seemed to Moser that there was a limit to the number of tourists the natural environment could accommodate without giving way under the onslaught. He thought the Gurglers needed to reactivate their latent knowledge of limits so they could plan to skirt them. Unlike the Gurglers, who are walled in their valley and tend to take cues only from one another, Moser was traveling the world with an open mind. Early in the 1970s the International Biological Program, which had funded his research on Nebelkogel, was focusing on another and, from a human standpoint, more directly relevant endeavor—the Man and Biosphere (MAB) program. Its goal was to discover the results of the eternal give-and-take between people and their natural environment. One segment of the project, MAB Six, as it is known, dealt with mountain ecosystems. Here Moser found his niche. Between the Alpine Research Station's capacity to monitor the fragile ecosystem that was the Gurglers' natural world and the Gurglers' full-throttled enthusiasm to manipulate the valley to serve their own ends, Obergurgl was a perfect natural laboratory for such research.

In 1972, at a tundra-research conference in Fort Collins, Colorado, Moser found some of his own colleagues trying to adapt a new, computerized method to the study of ecological systems. He had heard talk about a new idea expounded by Dennis and Donella Meadows in their new book, *Limits to Growth*. The book had appeared that year, and its basic contention was that nothing can expand indefinitely; expansion must stop when the resources that allow the growth—food, energy, even space—are used up. *Limits to Growth* used computer modeling to prove its point. Moser began to think it might be possible to construct a computer model for Obergurgl.

Moser returned to the University of Innsbruck a new, if somewhat naive, proselytizer for the technique. "[We can] put variables in the machine and, just as in a game, change some of the factors. Then, using this information, we can create new theories," he told his colleagues. "We might find the machine is right!"

"This is American junk," some of his colleagues told him. Others were more enthusiastic. This particular use of computers was new to Innsbruck, but the researchers were willing to try it. They soon found, however, that the real work would be performed by humans, not by the computer. In order to produce its information, the computer would require them to draw up a conceptual map—a model—of Obergurgl. The conceptual map would include all the factors that have to do with land use around Obergurgl—everything from the cost of building hotels to the avalanche rate, from the eating habits of the wild chamois to the spending habits of the Germans.

The model would be a printed guide to how the separate factors that make up the Obergurgl system are connected. For example, the number of people in the village is directly connected to the number of hotels constructed, and eventually the pathway loops again to connect both these factors with the number of people employed in the tourism industry. The model would be used to reveal how seemingly discrete factors have an effect upon one another. Numbers derived by research would be used to weight the importance of connections the modelers would draw between the different factors. Because the importance of each factor varies over time as it interacts with other factors, this weighting can not be accomplished coherently without a computer; the process is too complex for the human mind, which seems to have difficulty conceiving of feedback loops.

A feedback loop is a repetitive pattern that amplifies or diminishes over time. Moser's notion that tourism kills tourism is a good example. Obergurgl was expanding to accommodate more tourists not just once, but again and again, by building more hotels and more lifts. But each time Obergurgl expanded it lost more of the pristine quality that attracted the tourists. Other problems might come into play—the walking trails might become overcrowded, paper litter tossed away by careless picnickers might increase, visitors would be frustrated by crowded parking lots. Moser was afraid the villagers might be pushing the valley unwittingly toward a point of no foreseeable return.

It wouldn't be the first time. Systems had collapsed before in the high Gurgler valley. But time doesn't stop when a feedback loop collapses; another kind of balance is always reached. For example, aside from the forest the children had saved, the slopes around Obergurgl had been nearly denuded of trees, and the situation was similar all down the Oetztal. The last of the great forests was cut or burned by pasture-seeking nomads by A.D. 850, about the time Charlemagne was taking the emperor's crown in Paris. Eleven hundred-odd years later, the forests have not regenerated, for a number of reasons. Slow erosion has taken all but a few inches of the soil that covers the rock. Summer grazing, thin hillside soil, and extremely high ground temperatures (up to 70 degrees C, almost 160 degrees F, in the summer) discourage the growth of new trees. Those that do take root face winters with heavy snows that slide slowly downhill, dragging the saplings from their anchorage with their insistent weight. Grasses, on the other hand, accommodate themselves to the thin soil and heavy snowfall.

The forests were originally cleared for pasture, and though the grassland that took over from the forest was stable, it was less biologically productive than the system that preceded it. (Biological productivity is simply the measure of the accumulation of living mass supported on any patch of earth; a forest invariably beats a tundra.) The sheep are disappearing, the ungrazed grass is growing long, and once again a feedback loop is collapsing, with some dire consequences: on short grass the snow falls between the blades and anchors snugly; on long grass the snow anchors at random, penetrating between some of the blades and forming freestanding bridges over the rest. With only sporadic grounding to bind it, the snow is more likely to avalanche. A seemingly minor event—a change in the weather or a chamois wandering over a ridge—can trigger it. With the spring thaw, the properties of the snow change. Wet snow compacts as it melts, and refreezes at night. Where the snow has found anchorage between clumps of grass, its grip turns to ice. The grasses are yanked free, exposing the bare soil to the torrential runoff.

Entire sections of hillside lose their grounding and slip-slide downslope, like midnight drunks.

* * * * *

As long as they maintained control over the pastures, change-overs in vegetable dynasties didn't concern the Gurglers. The hoteliers were satisfied as long as the supply of tourists continued to increase. Moser's alarms sounded whenever he saw the people take actions that detracted from the blue-ribbon quality of the valley's natural world. The two aims didn't always mesh. Moser realized that his first job was to convince the Gurglers that they had a problem.

In 1973, Moser invited the Gurglers to a special meeting. A couple of dozen people found him in the meeting room of a Gasthaus, standing in front of a blackboard and drawing an isosceles triangle. It was Obergurgl's first introduction to computer modeling. Moser explained that his triangle represented the relationships among the demands of the most important systems in the valley.

"You have a landscape here," he told them. "You have a village, a place that is nice and beautiful. You have a lot of quality. Then a few outsiders discovered it. Attracted by this landscape, they went into your village and into your surroundings as the first tourists." At the corners of the triangle he drew a *Q*, for quality, and a *T*, for tourism. "Your poor grandfathers here, they soon discovered that the tourists had money in their pockets. And what did they do with this money? They reinvested it in the valley. They built some Alpine huts. They started some hotels to serve the tourists." Moser put an *E*, for economy, in the third corner. The number of visitors increased, as everyone knew, and so Moser added a *V* in a little balloon above the *T*. "This worked together nicely for a hundred years," Moser concluded. "This is a simple model of Obergurgl."

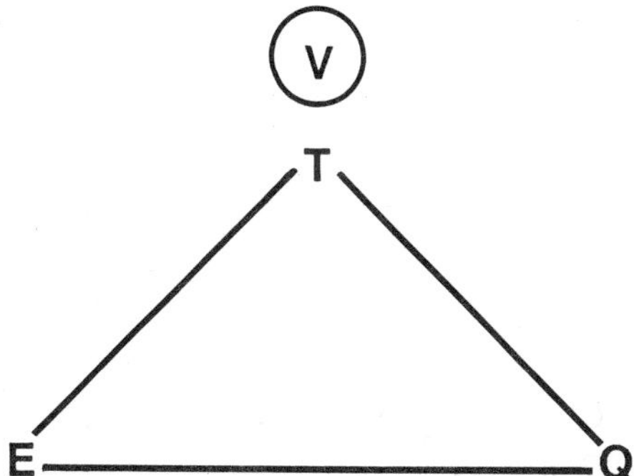

At the next meeting, Moser demonstrated the effects of manipulating this system. "We now have a much bigger source of vacationers," he said. "We have thousands and thousands of tourists. We have a beautiful economy. Now let us ask the question, 'What happens to the landscape, and to the quality of life in this town?' There's no doubt about it. If you overdo it on this side," and he indicated the top of the model, pointing to the circles of Visitor, Tourism, and Economy, "then you reduce this side to zero." He erased the circle containing the lone *Q*. "Soon you can forget about this nice hundred-year-old cycle of things helping one another. I think this is the truth," he told them, "that we cannot develop infinitely. There is a limit somewhere."

Moser understood that what motivates these people is their families' welfare. When they build, the Gurglers are building for the future, for the security of their children. When women meet on the village streets they don't ask about one another's children; they ask, "How's business?" To them it's the same thing. They strive to provide their children with the opportunity to stay in Obergurgl. If someone has a bit of land secure from avalanches and a few *schillinge* in the bank, he will build a hotel for one of his children. Those who have no property in the village are forced to leave town. The prosperity of their land and their children—and the Gurglers have a fierce attachment to both—depends on tourism.

"I'm not here to make friends. That's not my job," Moser insisted. "But you are probably doing the wrong thing. Maybe not one single tourist will come again if you continue to develop." If the tourists were going to stop coming, even for reasons that were then clear only to Moser, then there was truly something to work on. Finally, one man asked him, "Well, what do you want us to do?"

"It's not so difficult," Moser replied. "We just have to change this simple-minded attitude we have in this country. We read in the newspapers, 'In our town we have one million overnights.' This competition makes the deadly circle you see in this model. But we have to see reality as reality is. We need to know this *Q*, how stable it is, how it functions. We have to investigate our resources, our water, our green land. Then we can steer our development. We have to gather information about how to keep the quality and the tourists in a nice relationship with the economy. Here I can offer you some help from science. We can analyze this system. We can ask questions."

The project would be funded by the Austrian MAB Six program and the International Institute for Applied Systems Analysis, which had recently been established in the Schloss Laxenburg, near Vienna. The villagers need invest nothing but some time, he told them. Gotthard Scheiber and Adi Fender, another hotelier, were chosen to represent the villagers' interests at a special meeting at Laxenburg. Peter Scheiber, a cousin who had grown up in Gotthard's home and was now an official with the Austrian Department of Tourism, was also invited. Seven scientists from Austria, another from France, one from Germany, and one from Italy were invited to Laxenburg. Five members of the Institute of Animal Resource Ecology at the University of British Columbia in Vancouver, a group that had amassed a good deal of experience in ecological computer modeling, flew in. They met for five days in May in the old palace.

Everyone contributed, each according to his expertise: water supply, energy supply, parking spaces, land use, tourist capacity, ski-lift waiting time, building cost, population size, wages, savings, hay production, alpine-meadow biomass production, avalanche rate, forest cover, chamois population, and more. Adi Fender and Gotthard Scheiber discovered their own knowledge to be encyclopedic, and still they were kept on the telephone, ringing up Broser and the other farmers back home to ask how many animals they each had and how much the animals ate. Everything that could be imagined to be relevant to Obergurgl's economic and environmental health was included.

By the third day, the Canadians had assembled a model for everyone to contemplate. The bare-bones, nonmathematical map looked like the one on the following page.

When the modelers ran the computer model under the assumption that habitat diversity was indeed a measure of the quality of the valley and did make a difference to tourists, they found the model spilling out the classic feedback loop: fewer tourists would come if the natural quality of the valley was poor. Yet the links between the two elements were not where stress was occurring. Upon examining their data, the modelers honestly doubted this scenario of environmental overuse leading to decreased tourism would materialize in Obergurgl.

A bigger surprise was brewing. Just by looking at the way the model was emerging, the modelers were beginning to suspect that the most important element in this model had very little to do with the environmental factors that had been Moser's concern, and everything to do with the villagers' main concern. Before any of the numbers were fed into the computer, they saw something that had been apparent to neither Moser nor the villagers: they could see that Obergurgl definitely had a limit to its growth. That limit was the same one that the Gurglers had

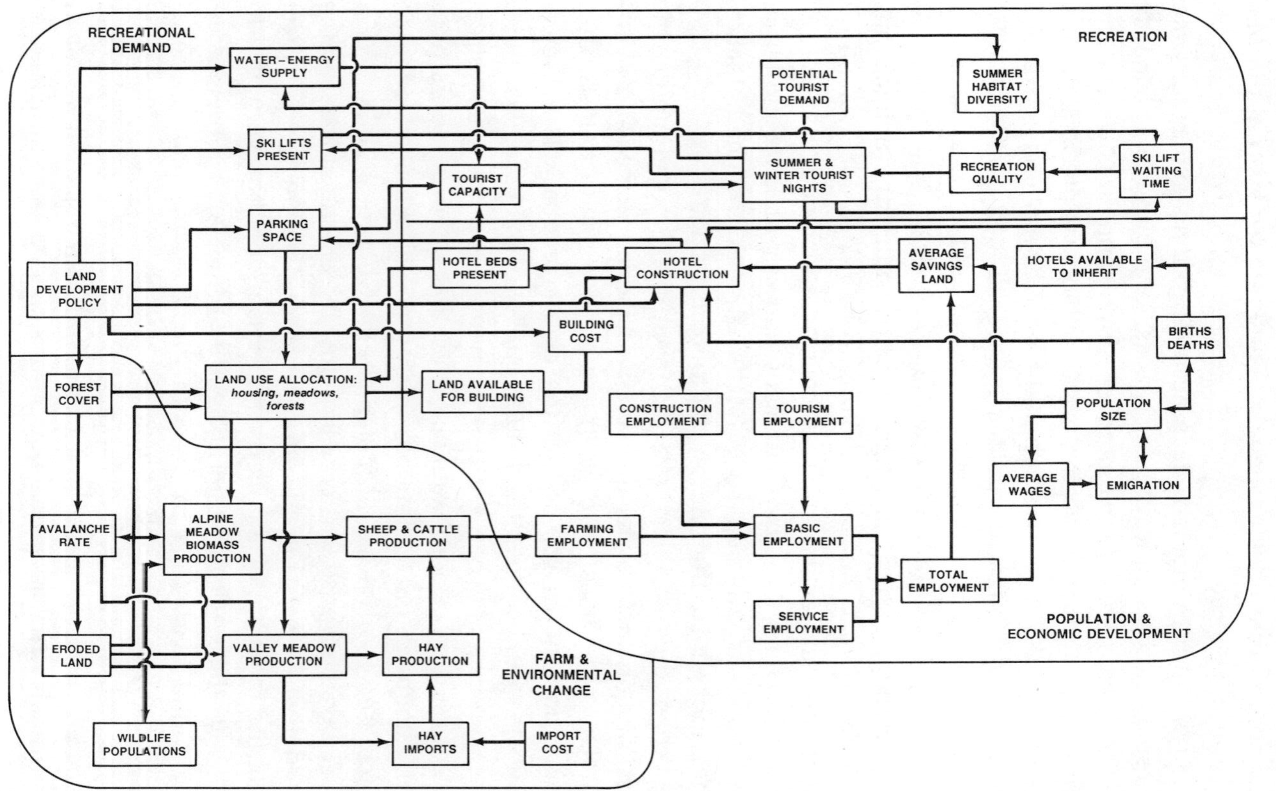

Reprinted with permission by International Institute for Applied Systems Analysis, Laxemburg, Austria.

come up against 122 years before, when they outlawed marriage. What would stop the village from growing would be the simple eventuality of having too many people and not enough land.

The modelers had assumed, on the advice of Scheiber and Fender, that only villagers' sons would be building hotels. The number of villagers available to build hotels was the same as the number of male Gurglers who didn't already own a hotel. It takes about seven years of work, Scheiber and Fender reported, for a young man to save enough money to build a hotel from winter work as a ski instructor and summer work as a construction worker or field hand. The modelers counted the number of male children in the village and divided by the amount of land that was still available. There was room for only about twenty new hotels, they figured, as they pored over a map of the valley and marked off the lots not threatened by avalanche, if the regulations about site sizes didn't change. Now, said the modelers to the scientists, the Gurglers, and Moser, you can actually point to this six-year-old boy today growing up in Obergurgl and you can say to him, "You will be the last person ever to build a hotel here and, if circumstances don't change too much, you will build the last hotel in 1996."

In the year that followed, while the town rang with the sound of this portcullis slamming down, the scientists went to work on the complex problem of measuring everything in the model as accurately as possible. "Eroded land," for example, which sits in the bottom left-hand corner of the model above, was assumed to be the result of several, often concurrent and interrelated factors: for example, the number of sheep on the alpine meadows and the erosion that might be expected due to overgrazing, or the number of summer and winter visitors who hiked and skied. (Gotthard Scheiber and Adi Fender ventured their doubts that winter tourists and cows had any effect on erosion at all. They still doubt it.) Each factor's contribution to erosion was estimated and assigned a numerical value, more or less arbitrarily, but it soon became clear that the scientists needed to study the problem more quantitatively. In fact, erosion soon emerged as the single most important element in need of further study. As Moser, with his little blackboard picture, had implied, the erosion rate could be linked to recreational quality and tourist visits; but connecting lines to boxes did not tell the modelers how the summer tourists actually reacted to their natural surroundings, and so they could make no accurate predictions. Because of this, Moser's original notion could neither be proved nor disproved.

The scientists sought to find out how the plants of the area withstood being trampled by hikers, or being sliced by ski edges when the snow was thin, or being crushed by the tractor-like snowcats that daily trundled their weight over the south side of the valley. The prime study site was the Hohe Mut, a peak behind the village just to the east of the Gurgler glacier, where Hans Falkner had built a restaurant. For twenty years the ski lift to the Hohe Mut had run in the summer as well as the winter. A university botanist, Georg Grabherr, marked off small slices of trail near the Hohe Mut, foot by foot, and literally counted the number of times a human foot struck the ground in each section. He dug up the plants adjoining the path and measured their roots. He measured the volume of the soil on the path, checking the natural garden for damage, gauging the cumulative effect as the footsteps thudded over the path.

Grabherr found that alpine lichens are destroyed in one trample, or a high wind. The mosses couldn't withstand more than twenty-five hikers passing over them. Half of the tansy by the trails disappeared under fifty footsteps a day. The parsleys held out with half their bulk intact until the crowd reached 150 foot steps a day. The stalwart alpine sedge, *carex curvula,* was the hardest to stamp out.

The evolutionary response of sedge to severe surface cold

and an uncertain growing season had been to give up seeding altogether. It spread rhizomes beneath the thin soil surface instead, and these runners rose blindly to the surface and again shot forward. Above the ground the sedge is but one of many plants; below, it's king, and its roots make up four-fifths of the underground world. Thus, it was discovered that sedge rhizomes and roots are the soil's strongest protection against rain, wind, and the spring thaw.

On the upslope side of the path, where the earth had been trampled hard by the soles of feet that the scientists tallied individually, the sedge was making a foray over the dirt. Like an underground army, the rhizomes were progressing downhill, swallowing an inch of path edge each summer. But on the downhill side of the path the sedge was in retreat. Conquered by feet and erosion, it was losing territory thirty times faster than the upslope plants were gaining it. Between the two lines of attack and retreat the hikers paced over the path, enjoying the view of what they assumed was a timeless meadow.

The entomologists followed the botanists, stooping to lay their small netted traps on chosen spots. Where the plants had been trampled there were fewer dead leaves and roots to feed bacteria and worms. This meant less food for the insects. The researchers' small blue notebooks recorded half as many insects on the much-used ski slopes and high walking paths as on the meadows reserved for grazing. On the heavily used slope where the ski school trained its beginners, the summer count was 100 beetles per ten square feet; higher on the slope, where the beginners feared to go, the entomologists counted 1,000 beetles in an equivalent space. The biologists found 160 earthworms per ten square feet in the untouched sward; in ten square feet of ski slope, where the snow had been smoothed and skied and smoothed and skied for thirty years, they found only one. It seemed as if bit by bit the life in the meadows above Obergurgl was being invisibly erased.

Next, meteorologist Michael Kuhn measured the microclimate of a corrected hillside from the surface of the mountain up through the clear air to a height of five inches. He found a microclimate of Sahara-like severity—a five-inch-high desert. In the heat poured out by the sun and reflected by the bare gravel, even the sedge failed to thrive. Because plants cycle water from rootlet to leaf in order to regulate their internal temperatures, on the corrected slopes the plants that tried to pioneer lost all their water to the air just in the effort to stay cool. They wilted, dried up, and disappeared.

In time, most of the landscape would be able to recover. Given thirty years of peace, the sedge might overgrow the trail. The worms would turn out again in numbers if given fifty to seventy-five years. The insects would come back in a few weeks. But the damage was worst on the ski slopes, where bulldozers had performed what was called "topographic corrections," ironing out the bumps and hollows of millions of years of geological activity. Ten and twenty years after the slopes had been corrected, nothing was growing. The barren slopes, with no vegetation to hold them, began to push downhill.

At the prodding of the Alpine Research Station scientists, an attempt was made to stabilize the slope. With enough fertilizer, grass can be encouraged to grow. Gotthard Scheiber channeled $60;000 of the village tourist association's funds to mend the damage. Some of the *pistes* were seeded with rye, but the scientists saw this as only temporary; the grass would protect the ground, but it would not replace the original meadow. Rye, a lower-altitude grass, would not go to seed on the high slopes. In five years these grasses would fail. The original vegetation, said the Innsbruck botanists, wouldn't return before the year 2000.

* * * * *

But the villagers were not convinced. Gotthard said he had

never heard the summer tourists complain about what he saw as apron-sized patches of topographic correction. The bare spaces weren't spreading. Obergurgl wasn't about to slide over the hill into Italy because of the work of a few heavy machines. Mostly the Gurglers wondered what all this fuss had to do with them. There wasn't a skiable slope in the entire Oetztal, from Obergurgl to the Inn, that hadn't been smoothed; there wasn't a hikeable trail in the Tyrol that didn't turn to mud when it rained. "Do you think you can bring your model here and tell us what to do?" Erich Scheiber, Gotthard's brother, asked Moser. Broser, more gentle, said, "This will mean nothing to us unless you bring it into our living rooms."

Moser was learning, belatedly, about the most useful function of the model. He had envisioned a series of exponentially expanding models: for Obergurgl, for the Tyrol, for the Alps. He had hoped that, once he understood how outside forces affect ecosystems and had these humming along in one corner of the model, he could expand the same model to cover all the mountains. Now the vision was deflected, and Moser realized that the model's real power was in its ability to generate discussion.

In May of 1975, a year after the first model had been hammered out at Laxenburg, some members of the modeling team reassembled in the village. With a desk-top computer to back them up, they demonstrated their methods to the Gurglers. An assumption that the Gurglers couldn't ignore was that when no new hotels could be built their children would have to leave town. Neither could the Gurglers ignore the by now obvious conclusion that there would come a time, sooner rather than later, when there would be no room to build new hotels.

The modelers advised the Gurglers to direct their children into trades not dependent upon tourism, and the Gurglers took note; but about the health of the meadows they worried little. "Moser is a radical," one farmer argued. "He is afraid that tourism is taking the farming away from Obergurgl." This man's farm was secure for another generation; his second son was ready to take it over, and the son could be trusted to mind his pastures well. But the establishment of 1996 as the date when hotel-building sites were likely to be used up had disturbed everyone. With Gotthard Scheiber as the main proponent, there was a long and difficult discussion about putting a limit on building in Obergurgl. It seemed wise to stop building long enough to think about which of each farmer's growing children would really want to stay home and run a hotel. No one was willing to sign anything; there were no referenda. But there was an informal agreement among the people to stop building hotels.

Because their hotels are their livelihood, the Gurglers had to find another method to increase their profits. They decided to concentrate on attracting a wealthier clientele. Sölden, a village further down the Oetztal, had opted to attract the masses. Skiers could find cheaper accommodations and meals there; often people would come in overnight, or for an afternoon. Obergurgl decided to avoid the masses and upgrade their accommodations in order to attract the kind of skier who would stay a week or two and pay more for comfort. In this way, the Gurglers wouldn't have to build more hotels in order to take in more money.

So began another round of construction. This one actually decreased the number of rooms in some of the large hotels, as walls were removed to make room for individual showers and baths. Within a few years, every room in some hotels had its own bath, and hoteliers no longer had to wait for some less particular visitor to come to lodge in the more plebeian, bathless rooms.

The agreement to limit growth was so informal that some Gurglers deny it was ever made, but between 1975 and 1982 no new hotels were built in the village. The valley thrived. The model had suggested that a way to measure skier satisfaction would be to clock waiting time at the ski lifts. In an article in a

German financial magazine, *Kapital,* that rated all the ski resorts in Europe by waiting time, Obergurgl was rated second in all of Europe—much to the glee of Hans Falkner, ski-lift-company president. Obergurgl stopped growing and started improving, in their own way confirming Moser's original notions about *Q, V, T,* and *E.*

* * * * *

For a while it seemed as if the talk that had followed the modeling project had kindled a new land-use ethic, a conscientious trusteeship of the valley among the people. Not only was the building of new hotels shelved, but plans to lengthen the little road that now dead-ends on the far side of town so that it led right up to the Gurgler glacier were dropped. The town of Sölden had, with great trouble and expense (and, in retrospect, with very little return on its investment), established a summer skiing area on a nearby glacier. The Gurglers had been thinking of doing the same thing to give a boost to their summer business, but the plans were never carried out. Some say this was because of Moser's timely education of the villagers, but others claim the plans were dropped because the skiing was no good on the glacier there anyway.

In 1981 the entire southern ridge of the Oetztaler Alps, an area six by nine miles, was put off limits to further development. It's now a *Ruhezone*, a quiet zone, a kind of nature preserve or national park. The Gurglers couldn't build ski lifts on that side of the valley now even if they wanted to. Since a similar proposal to set aside land near Salzburg has been blocked by the Salzburgers for over twenty years, some say the establishment of a *Ruhezone* was allowed in Obergurgl because of the Gurglers' more enlightened ecological attitudes. On the other hand, others note the number of avalanches that occur there regularly and point out that the skiing was not good up there anyway.

One clear result of the model was that new attention was directed to the farmers. It at last became apparent to the hoteliers that Obergurgl's summer beauty required care, and that care of the land doesn't come free as the winter snow. The tourist board started paying the farmers a "beauty tax" to encourage them to continue to hay the meadows, even though it is easier and now cheaper for them to import hay than it is to hire the labor to mow their own.

Many of the alternative land-use plans the modelers used in order to produce possible futures for Obergurgl have now become national policy. The national government, for reasons of safety and economy, issued a directive requiring natural-hazards zoning. Having found itself building avalanche gates to protect buildings that were being erected in known danger zones, the government drew up zoning maps showing the areas where building is no longer allowed. Obergurgl's map is as colorful as a carnival, full of red—indicating a known avalanche area—and yellow—denoting a more uncertain danger. Much of the green—indicating safety—is already built upon. Now there are only a few places, fewer even than the modelers had assumed, where new hotels may be built.

Some of the farmers complain of the restriction on what they're allowed to do with their land. They blame Gotthard Scheiber and his support of the model's results for this.

"Sometimes, after some drinks, they come up to me and say, 'Gotthard, you messed this up down there in Laxenburg. Why can't I build for my son?' " Scheiber reports. For the moratorium in building had a social effect that no one had foreseen: the process of redistribution of wealth in Obergurgl is now frozen. There are no new fortunes to be made in hotel building. The great families have remained so, and the small families resent this. They resent Scheiber and they resent Moser.

Moser made a gallant attempt to keep the people of the village talking to one another. In 1979 he founded a men's choir. Its members still meet on Wednesday evenings in the church. But what was really needed was a constant presence, and Moser was no zoo-keeper. His work in Obergurgl was completed and had been noted internationally. Moser received an excellent offer to move to Edmonton, Alberta, to become a botany professor at the University of Edmonton. He accepted.

* * * * *

After Moser left, Gotthard Scheiber was heard to say, "And now he is there, but we are still here." In 1980, he brought in a crew to blast out a section of the rocky Oxenkopf. He needed a hole by the side of the road in order to lay the foundation for what he intended to be the largest hotel yet built in Obergurgl. The lot had originally been sold to a good friend of the owner, a ski-lift operator of twenty years who was tired of commuting to work and wanted to live and start his own business in the village. The man's request for permission to build had been turned down by the zoning board on the grounds that the site was in a beauty zone where building is not allowed. When Gotthard bought the land he immediately began blasting, without permission.

The villagers haven't yet reached a consensus about Gotthard's action. Herlinde Broser thinks it isn't a bad idea. The hotel will be of excellent quality, she knows, and it will attract the kind of tourist Obergurgl prefers. Frau Broser knows how to take the long view. She was the first villager to act on the future predictions of the Obergurgl model; although she and her husband own thirty hectares of land, her children have all been sent to school in Innsbruck to learn trades.

For the last twenty years, village children have grown up expecting to run hotels. The other jobs have always been taken by outsiders—800 of them each winter season. There had never before been a question of a shortage of work for the children of the Gurglers.

Now that the farm children of a decade ago are beginning to start their own families, a housing crisis is emerging, too. One man, whose wife is expecting their first child, has been trying to get permission to build on land above Gotthard's excavation for six years. "The great families can do everything here. The small families can do nothing," he says. This isn't entirely true. For the new Scheiber hotel to be built, it must have access to water. The springs are on the hillside, on farm land. Pipes would have to be laid from the springs over a meadow, on farm land. So far, the farmers have turned down Gotthard's request to pipe water to his new site.

Much of the resentment has come because Gotthard was the most enthusiastic proponent of limiting growth. The farmer's options were cut off by this limit, explains another hotelier, just at the time when the farmers had enough money to make large investments for their children. So when they see new property going to a man who already owns one large hotel and several restaurants, the farmers balk.

"Of course there will be some struggle now about who is getting what," says Moser, who keeps up with Obergurgl from his faraway prairie home in Edmonton. "But Gotthard wouldn't have had any problems with his Oxenkopf idea in the 1960s."

In this village, money-making still seems the only game in town, and the model has become a dead issue. "I know what the model is, but I don't know how it worked," says Herlinde Broser. Another hotelier says she has had the booklet explaining the model, eighty pages modestly entitled *Alpine Areas Workshop: May 13-17, 1974,* beside her bed for years. It's a fixture on her night table. Now, after a hard day at work, she drops off to sleep just looking at the cover; the book has never been opened.

"Nobody expected a general and total end to growth," says

Moser. "But these questionings brought about a very important and basic change: a very solid land-use plan limiting further growth very effectively and stabilizing the system. The Ruhezone Oetztaler Alpen is such a wonderful and great success, the inhabitants will probably only discover the benefits in the next decades."

At Gotthard Scheiber's suggestion, Obergurgl's advertising bills the village as "The Model Place of UNESCO," and the town has gained much publicity from the project. *Alpine Areas Workshop: May 13-17, 1974,* sits on the large lobby desk of Gotthard's hotel, like a paperback Gideon's Bible, and it's well thumbed. Among the tourists at least, he claims, it's the most popular book in town. Once again, it seems the Gurglers have found a way to wring a golden egg out of the snow goose.

CHAPTER FOUR

The Solar-Heated, Biogas-Powered Cheese Factory

DURING his assignment in Nepal, Andres Fritschy spent many of his evenings in an abandoned tree nursery in the company of two rats and a large green snake. Res, as he was known, was an agronomical engineer with the Swiss Association for Technical Assistance (SATA). He filled the long evenings with paperwork, preferring not to go outside at night for fear of falling over the cliff left by the area's latest landslide, which had come within inches of the nursery building. He had been sent to Nepal partly to deal with the landslide problem; and when the solar-heated, biogas-powered cheese factory hadn't worked either, and the lines on his daily production charts inclined ever downward, he wrote impassioned letters to SATA's Zürich headquarters. His superiors told him to stop complaining and try harder.

There had been much to complain about in Zürich, too. By the time he went to Nepal at the age of thirty, Fritschy was a disillusioned veteran of the anti-nuke and pro-ecology movements. When he joined SATA's Nepal development staff it had been with the hope of helping to modernize Nepal in a way he could reconcile with his principles. Now, thanks to SATA, he was sitting 6,000 feet up a mountain, the only German speaker within two days' walk, and within deafening earshot of over a hundred pigs. The pigs, fed on whey, were supposed to excrete the raw material that was supposed to stock a methane tank that was supposed to fuel the flames under boilers that were supposed to heat milk to make cheese.

They didn't. Res Fritschy often wondered what he was doing in the middle of Nepal, weighing pig dung.

The story begins several years before Fritschy's arrival. The solar-heated, biogas-powered cheese factory, a series of low buildings draped down the side of a mountain in Jugepani Pauwa, had been built to manufacture Swiss-style cheese. Pauwa is three days' walk southeast of Kathmandu, 6,000 feet above sea level, and six-sevenths of a mile above the bottom of the nearest river canyon. At the top of the slope, a footpath zigzagged back and forth along the ridgeline. Below the path, on a small terrace cut into the hill, were the cheese storage rooms, the cheese factory, and the dairyman's home. These solid, stone buildings sat on foundations of poured concrete. Their shiny aluminum roofs reflected bright silver toward the sky, even on cloudy days. The piggery, made of stone in the Swiss manner and as solid as the dairy, sat on the terrace below these buildings. Below it, a mud-walled building housed three huge methane tanks. Finally, on the lowest terrace of all, the last before the land dropped too steeply to terrace, there was the tree nursery where Res now lived. This was a building of whitewashed mud, low ceilings, and few windows, with a narrow ladder connecting the two stories. Of all the dairy outbuildings, this one alone was built in the Nepali style.

Jugepani, which means "leech water," is a valley with a full subscription to all of Nepal's long list of shortcomings, and although a single leech up a nostril can kill a cow, the leeches are the least of it. In all respects Pauwa is an ecological and social disaster area. It is one of the poorest areas in a very poor country. Here, most of the farms don't cling to the steep mountainsides—the only ten hectares of flat land in this 1,600-hectare district are at the bottom of the steep river canyons. But the flat land moves around a lot, washed out here and deposited there at the river's whim. After a rainy season, men gather in the river to heave huge boulders into a line, a sort of dike they hope will divert the river away from their rice paddies. After a good storm, the river can wash the boulders away as if they were styrofoam. Upslope, where at least the villagers don't have to worry about getting washed away, there's no water at all: the springs there dry up soon after the rains. Many of the villagers live a one- or two-hour walk from the nearest running stream.

The summer rainy season brings another set of problems. All this water means serious erosion, and soil disappears from these hills like fat off a starving man. In the soft limestone and gneiss soil, new gullies begin every time it rains. There is very little tree cover; the terraces where trees might have grown have long since been abandoned, because the soil was washed away just a few years after the terraces were built. Placed as they were on ground that slopes at a more-than-30-degree angle, they were impossible to maintain. These steepest of slopes had only been terraced in the first place because one family in five in Pauwa doesn't own enough decent land to feed itself. The people have no choice but to push the limit.

Crops don't grow easily, either. Local corn is subject to attacks of stem borer. Fields are raided by roaming cows—national and religious laws prohibit the slaughter of cows too old to give milk, so they are allowed to roam freely through fields and terraces until they die—and plundered by roving bands of wild monkeys—sacred to the local people and therefore immune from retaliation. Even the children are unusually fragile; because of bad water, many of them die of complications begun by diarrhea before the age of five. The diarrhea comes from drinking unclean water, often the only kind available. It is easily treated by oral rehydration, but in Pauwa there's no doctor, no medical information, and no books about diarrhea, since 98 percent of the women and 80 percent of the men are illiterate. The few educated people, mostly high-caste Hindus, don't mix with the lower castes, so information doesn't spread within the community. Even so, high-caste and low-caste mothers alike are not easily convinced that babies whose stools are practically liquid can be treated with yet more water.

The south- and southeast-facing slopes in Pauwa look more desertlike every year, partly because of the farming and partly because of the farm animals. The 520 inhabitants there keep about a dozen animals each, animals that require enough food to make the farmer who carries it home to them resemble a walking haystack.

Ten years ago, all that Pauwa had going for it was a fast-talking and influential politician who obtained loans from the Agricultural Development Bank of Nepal so that the local people could purchase new, high-yield buffalo. These animals, the ponderous dusky-brown water buffalo of India, with coat hanger hips and swept-back horns, can give up to five litres of rich, sweet milk a day. The Nepali variety often give but one or two. Villagers took advantage of the opportunity, borrowed a bit of the buffalos' price from the local moneylenders, and walked their new crossbreeds up over the hills from the plains of India.

The buffalo deal was welcomed by the people as a way to make money, but the scheme had not been designed with the farmers in mind. It had been the local moneylenders who prevailed over the local politician to provide Pauwa's people with a source of income. It is so hard to find a way to make money in this region that the people have to borrow from moneylenders when they need clothes, pots, seed corn, or even rice. The moneylenders, who have been known to charge up to 50 percent interest but are as dependent on the villagers as the villagers are on them, looked for some way to help the people pay off their debts.

Pauwa is only a two- or three-day walk from India, where the country is flat, where there are roads and trains and buses, and where trade is possible. Traders have always come to Nepal's hills to buy low-priced goods to resell at a profit in India, and Pauwa's regular trading item, the one that brought what money there was to the region, was the local cooking staple, *ghee*—clarified butter—which doesn't spoil in the heat and can be transported for long distances. The milk from the high-yield buffalo was to be churned into butter, made into *ghee*, and sold to the traders, thus providing the farmers with cash to pay back both the moneylenders and the Agricultural Development Bank. The logic of the plan seemed flawless. The people at the Agricultural Development Bank counted the number of buffalo they had sponsored, multiplied by five quarts a day, and listed Pauwa as an area of "milk surplus," with a high potential of expanding the cottage-based *ghee* industry.

* * * * *

The buffalo-buying scheme was the first of what was to become a series of Band-Aid cures for Pauwa's problems. In 1975, India was blessed with plenty of rain, but not too much, at the right time. The buffalo in the plains for once found plenty of forage. Lowland *ghee* production rose, and its price in the far-away hills of Nepal fell drastically. When the value of Pauwa milk fell, the farmers and moneylenders found themselves short of cash. Thinking they might solve the problem by buying yet more buffalo, they appealed to a government organization, the Dairy Development Corporation (DDC), for help. What they got, once the DDC became involved, was a cheese factory.

The DDC had been founded by SATA in the 1950s to run the country's dairy industry, but it is now wholly owned by the Nepali government. The Swiss, who had sent expert advisors to Nepal even before the country was opened to Westerners in 1951, had in just a few years established a successful cheese industry there. In nine spots in Nepal's high pastures, cheese as it was made in Switzerland had begun to appear alongside the brown crumbly dehydrated milk called Tibetan cheese, which is not a cheese at all. Made with yak milk, it was similar to

Emmenthaler, though a bit more gamey. Nepalis couldn't afford the cheese—a kilo would cost the average person a week's wages. But the tourists, who bought all of it, thought it was delicious; so the people from this protein-poor region exported their most plentiful protein food to town for the consumption of foreigners. Still, the cheese was a valuable source of foreign exchange, and the DDC was looking for places to expand.

There were several obstacles. First, pasteurizing milk uses large quantities of firewood, and the regions around the cheeseries were being stripped; the growing season is short in the mountains, and trees grow slowly. Second, when pastures are snowed in, which they are for most of the winter in the high country, the yaks don't give enough milk to make cheese, so during the tourist-heavy winter months there was no fresh cheese at all. The apparent solution to both difficulties was to build cheeseries in the subtropical middle hills, the Mahabharat Lekh—but the primary milk animal there is the buffalo, not the yak. Buffalo milk is not the raw material of choice for cheese: the pasteurization process turns the milk bitter and ruins the cheese. The Swiss worried over the problem until 1974, when a SATA home experimenter developed a promising solution. It seemed as though a good cheese could be produced from buffalo milk if the milk were pasteurized at a slightly lower temperature than cow or yak milk. The cheesemakers at the DDC also reported success with the method, and the DDC began its search for a new cheesery site in the Mahabharat Lekh in earnest. The "milk surplus" area in Pauwa appeared a likely site, so land was found and transferred to the DDC and the cheesery was launched.

SATA agreed to help out in the establishment of the factory. The Swiss agency had by this time diversified into other fields besides dairying. Among other things, it established a corporation that manufactured small-scale water-powered generators. A World Bank report had estimated that Nepal, with its 20,000-foot elevation loss in just 50 miles, had the capacity to generate an impressive 83 million megawatts or more of hydroelectric power per year, and the government had made hydropower a priority. Because of the country's high erosion rates, however, large hydroelectric dams tended to catch tremendous amounts of silt in their reservoirs, which therefore filled twice as fast as their engineers had predicted. Medium-sized hydroelectric plants, on the other hand, the run-of-the-river type, would often lose turbines in raging floods. Small-scale generators, such as those produced with SATA's help, seemed a practical, inexpensive, and widely useful alternative—except that there were very few industries in the country, and even fewer in the hills, that actually needed electricity. The Pauwa cheese factory, which needs power to run steam boilers, seemed to SATA experts a good opportunity to test out small-scale hydropower. After years of heating milk for *ghee* production, the area was short of firewood anyway.

* * * * *

In October 1975, just after the monsoon, a team of SATA experts walked to Pauwa, looked at the Mamti Khola—the little river near the village—and figured out how many miles of wire would be needed to bring electricity from a small-scale generator in the river up to the cheesery. SATA agreed to provide the power to the dairy, and the DDC began to build it.

There was a catch, of course. If you have seen the monsoon in Pauwa, when ten inches of rain can fall in two hours, it is hard to believe the severity of the drought in the dry season. The springs simply disappear, and with them the rivers they supply. When a SATA social survey team walked to Pauwa a few months later, in the dry season, the Mamti Khola had disappeared. They realized, too late, that this was not a Swiss river with glaciers to feed it.

So the Swiss found themselves in Pauwa with no water and

no firewood. All they had was an agreement with the DDC that held them responsible for providing power for the cheese factory. These problems, and they were only the beginning, are a good example of the obstacles to successful industrialization in Nepal's hills. Industries fail because of the very conditions that make them necessary. Too many people are trying to live off the land and need an alternative, and while cottage industries seem a good solution they are too often just one more way to overuse the land.

Cheesemakers need to heat milk, and since a cheese factory in Pauwa was practically a fait accompli by now a source of heat had to be found. Hydroelectricity and firewood had to be ruled out. The milk could have been heated with kerosene-fired steam, but Pauwa was two days from the market, and importing kerosene on porters' backs would be expensive. There was some reluctance, too, to commit the cheesery to an imported energy source. Kerosene and foreign oil were therefore also out. Jugepani Pauwa's ridge is windy, but not dependably so. Photovoltaics were too expensive, clouds too certain. So relying on the weather was out. The alternative finally chosen was to make steam by burning methane, or biogas (*gobar* gas in the Nepali language) which is produced by the fermentation of ever-plentiful animal dung. There seemed no other choice.

* * * * *

Biogas was first introduced to Nepal by Father Bertrand Saubolle, a Jesuit who taught at St. Xavier's School for Boys, 15 miles outside Kathmandu. Of all his many good works in Nepal, his experience with biogas was among his favorites. "When I first came to Nepal," he said, "I realized that there was no coal, no kerosene, the firewood was disappearing at a tremendous rate. When I first came here in 1951, these hills were covered with forest. I saw the trees disappear."

In 1954, at an agricultural exhibition in India, Father Saubolle saw a demonstration model of a biogas plant. Although biogas had never really caught on in India, it caught on with Father Saubolle: "This is straight from heaven! This is the solution for Nepal! Why, there's cattle dung all over the place!" He started experimenting as soon as he got home. He had workmen dig a pit four feet wide and eight feet deep. While they were digging he took a basket to a nearby field and filled it with cow pies. When the pit was dug it was lined with mortar and lime. The workmen were directed to measure the dung in buckets, add an equal number of buckets of water, and stir the slop with a long bamboo pole until it had the consistency of cream. He had the pit capped with an upended oil drum.

After a couple of weeks the drum began to rise out of the pit. Father Saubolle collected the gas by opening a valve in the drum, then let it settle again. He looked for an audience and found the school carpenter, whom he took into the kitchen. The stove was burning a jet of ignited methane, odorless and almost invisible.

"Put your hand over the stove," he told the carpenter.

The carpenter obeyed, but pulled his hand quickly away.

"It's hot!" he said. "I don't know what it is, but it's hot."

Father Saubolle told him it came from the pit outside.

"Oh, you have filled the pit with kerosene?" he asked.

"No, it's water and cow dung."

The carpenter dashed out of the room. "Come, come quickly," he shouted. "Father's burning wet cow dung."

When the carpenter finally regained his manners, he said, "I have worked for colonels and I have worked for generals," he said, "but I have never seen anything as wonderful as this!"

It was not until almost twenty years later, when the price of oil skyrocketed in 1973, that the biogas plant generated that much excitement again. Father Saubolle was offered a seat on a government committee that arranged loans from the Agricultural

Development Bank to build biogas plants around the country. Two hundred were built. Eight years later, a follow-up survey found a third of them working and producing gas, a third ruined beyond repair, and a third abandoned for small and inexpensive repairs that any trained technician, had one been available, could have fixed.

Although the use of *gobar* gas has been dubbed "appropriate" technology, the system has often turned out to be inappropriate for reasons that no one could have foreseen. One community biogas plant was built in Lalitpur, outside Kathmandu, for example. This one wasn't for *gobar* (the literal translation is "cow dung"), but used human excrement, mostly from women, and some from their children. Each morning, as the sun rose, several hundred women would wander by ones and twos and threes to a small open field outside of town. Holding up their saris and stepping carefully, for this field had been used for a long, long time, they'd find a place to squat. Chattering and laughing with their friends, amid the flies and odor, they took their morning break. But now eighteen enclosed latrines were built in a circle. The women enjoyed this new privacy so much that more and more came. Soon the tank was loaded to capacity, but the gas that formed never burned: the methane concentration of the gas remained too low. The essential difference between cow dung, full of undigested, carbon-rich straw, and human excrement had not been fully appreciated. The tank's biological digesters were unable to produce methane on such a miserly quota of carbon. In the second place, there was too much water in the tank—Nepalis use water instead of toilet paper. The iron drum that held the gas corroded—human excrement and water produce a formidable amount of hydrogen sulphide. Finally, the caretaker's salary, made up of monthly contributions from the women, disappeared, and so did he. The plant fell into disrepair, leaving an overflowing slurry tank and eighteen latrines sitting in a circle in the field, and each morning the women still came.

A cheesemaker in SATA's employ, Beda Rust, was sent to Jugepani Pauwa. Since the Pauwa project was to be a simple biogas plant, a familiar technology with no moving parts, SATA assumed that the real challenge would now be to produce a marketable cheese from buffalo milk. Andreas Bachman, the SATA advisor who had lobbied in favor of biogas, had never actually built a biogas plant, had not toured the villages where the other plants had been built, and had no idea of all the ways in which the system could break down. Rust arrived in Nepal thinking he had only to help to produce a marketable cheese. He soon found, however, that the primitive cheesemaking technology in Pauwa was riddled with problems, and that with his expertise and some creativity, he could make an even greater impact.

The by-product of cheesemaking is whey, a translucent, high-protein, superbly skimmed milk from which all the solids have been removed by the cheesemaking process. Without a fast-running stream there was no easy way to get rid of it. The people of Pauwa didn't want it, even to feed the animals—they were convinced that all the nutrition had already been taken from it. One of the DDC's frustrations in Pauwa had been seeing all the skimmed milk, also a by-product of *ghee* production, being poured away. Back home in Switzerland, Rust's father had been a cheesemaker. He had kept pigs, and the pigs had eaten the whey. Rust looked at the Nepali mountains and dreamed of a system whereby pigs fed on whey would produce the dung to put slurry in the biogas tanks. He dreamed of importing huge fat Danish *Edelschwein*, noble pigs, which the villagers could eat when they grew too large; the local people wouldn't eat the long-legged skinny black pigs native to the area because they consume everything they scavenge, most of it unclean. Rust thought the local people should own the pigs, bring them feed, and later collect the used slurry for fertilizer (fermenting dung releases even more nitrogen than does raw dung and is therefore better in the fields). If Rust's father had used such a system in Switzerland it would have been remarkable. In Pauwa it would be nothing short of a miracle.

Pig dung would need warmth to ferment, at least 35 degrees C, and this was another challenge to Rust. Jugepani sits at 6,000 feet, and the winters are chilly and foggy. Two steep hours beyond Pauwa's main village Rust saw a former pasture transformed: there were eight new Nepali houses, the cheesery, and a building containing three vats for digesting dung, each the size of a large wine cask. There were three tea stalls. It was a boomtown, hill-style, where formerly there had been just a shepherd's hut. Now Rust added passive solar water heaters, thirty-two of them, to heat water that was piped into the insulated hut that housed the slurry tanks, thus warming them and enhancing the fermentation process.

Rust's plan seemed perfect. The villagers could come to the cheesery with their buffalo milk and pig feed and leave the cheesery with cash and fertilizer. The cheese factory would be self-sufficient, a model to be copied throughout Nepal. The pigs would eat the whey and make the dung that fueled the burners that heated the milk that made the cheese that left the whey that fed the pigs that lived in the house that Rust built. He called it an almost perfect example of complete recycling.

* * * * *

Almost at once, SATA's anxieties about the buffalo-milk cheese proved well founded. The heavy, cream-colored cheese wheels kept puffing up like overinflated tires, filled with the gases produced by contaminating bacteria. The looks didn't matter, but the bacteria left a disagreeable bitterness. Rust had to find a way to keep the milk cleaner. The area's general water shortage contributed to the lack of cleanliness. After spending hours toting water for humans and animals to drink, the village women never had the time to haul clean water to wash wooden milking buckets and buffalo udders. They didn't boil the water they used because of the firewood shortage. The people would dump the evening milk, which sat around all night, into the same wooden bucket as the fresh morning milk and carry it off to a milk-collection center, where all the milk, morning and evening, clean and contaminated, was poured into an aluminum milk can and carried up to Jugepani. It was a case of a few bad buckets spoiling the whole tank. But the only solution was to resolve the water shortage, and that required reforesting the hillsides so that the springs would run again.

So Beda Rust built a tree nursery, with the help of some villagers who were paying their taxes with labor. Soon he had 30 square miles of government-owned land planted with pine and leafy trees. Fines were levied on anyone caught chopping wood in the new forest. While the trees grew, Rust installed a water system, running polyurethane pipes from a collection tank above Pauwa through the village. Since this was his first attempt at this kind of engineering, he brought a friend to the site for a week to give him advice. But as the engineering problems with the biogas mounted and his own and his friend's skills proved unequal to the task, Rust finally convinced SATA of the need for technical assistance.

Enter, late in the fall of 1980, Res Fritschy. Besides himself and Rust, he found a Sherpa man, with his wife and children, who had been trained in Switzerland to make cheese. There were helpers for the dairy, and a junior technician in charge of pigs. The residences were equipped with solar-heated showers, a luxury not matched within a two-day walk. Beside the residential buildings was the cheesery, equipped with gleaming copper vats, a hand-cranked creamer, and a steam boiler that had been shipped to Kathmandu from Switzerland and delivered from there by helicopter. In the storage room the big cheeses sat on shelves. The piggery resounded with oinks and screams. The pig manure sat in vats warmed with solar water. The experiment seemed to be working. Fritschy expected to be back home within four months.

At first he concentrated on biogas, seemingly the knottiest problem. Rust thought he had solved the problem of the cheese blowing up, and his enthusiasm was contagious. The two men worked together for a few months, until Rust was promoted and reassigned to another SATA project in Pakistan, where he was to set up a dairy development agency. Soon after Rust departed, Fritschy saw the cheese cellar being cleared out—all the cheeses that had been made by Rust had spoiled and were being fed to the pigs. The buffalo-cheese problem had not been licked after all.

But Fritschy was curious. The biogas plant, he knew, was not yet operational, and he wondered how the milk had been heated in the meantime. The cheesemaker and his assistants explained that they had used firewood. This had been a giant step in the wrong direction. It was decided that, until the biogas plant was working, the steam would come from burning kerosene. It was therefore essential that Fritschy get the plant producing gas immediately: the kerosene was costing ten dollars a day, and no cheese had yet been sold.

The plant was designed to run downhill. Gutters from the piggery floor led to slurry pits, which fed dung into the three big digesting tanks. These emptied into drying pits, one below the next. Although the slurry pits were covered with glass and the building that enclosed the tanks was fully insulated with styrofoam sheeting, the temperature was still too low for the proper bacterial workout to take place. Rust had installed solar panels to help heat the tanks, but too often in Pauwa the sun just didn't shine. Instead of the optimal 35 degrees C, the digester tanks held steady at about 25 degrees C. Beda Rust had estimated that the cheesery could run on about 50 cubic feet of gas a day, but the actual requirement was closer to 80, and the tanks were only producing 15. Fritschy used the conditions he actually observed there to figure the plant's eventual output, and it came out to a disappointing 30 cubic feet a day. Efficiency, he thought gloomily, was something the Swiss couldn't export.

One way to improve the production of gas would be to produce more manure, and one way to get more manure from the pigs would be to feed them more. Whey alone turned out to be insufficient. Swiss veterinarians had predicted that the *Edelschwein* would die if whey comprised as much as 30 percent of their diet. The villagers weren't bringing pig feed to the dairy. They had a hard enough time gathering enough fodder to keep their buffalo producing milk, and to carry feed to the pigs up in Pauwa would have cost more hours per day than they had to spare. Feeding 120 pigs was turning out to be a huge expense to the dairy. The village head man who had assured Beda Rust that the people would gladly care for the pigs had merely done so to be polite, Res discovered.

The pigs had to eat. Potatoes were cheap, but they didn't work well; the skins went straight through the pigs and straight through the digester, clogging the pipes. The next easiest thing to feed the pigs was commercial feed, carried in burlap sacks all the way from Kathmandu but nonetheless inexpensive at just 3.5 rupees (about $.30) per pig per day. The commercial feed brought to Pauwa was the best on the market, a stew of meal, vitamins, minerals, and antibiotics. The antibiotics, like the potato skins, went straight through the pigs and into the digester, stopping the fermentation in the vats. Antibiotics are also antibiogas. The tanks had to be emptied and refilled, and the pigs went back to eating local produce.

The pigs soon went through the small surplus of corn and soybeans in the area—in a place where a fifth of the families cannot even achieve self-sufficiency, the people eat corn and soybeans too—and then corn and beans had to be brought from the Kathmandu valley. The price of these foods shot up quickly, but whereas the dairy could pay, the villagers couldn't. Porters bringing food destined for pigs were stopped and their loads confiscated, at intervals that corresponded with price fluctuations.

Still the amount of manure didn't increase. Because they ate only corn and beans, the impounded pigs were starved for minerals, so before it could be washed into the digester they ate their own dung. The whole recycling scheme was in tatters. Even the final, seemingly foolproof step—bringing the digested manure to the fields—didn't happen. Open-air pits had been built to hold the used slurry, and these had heads of suds, a sign that they were still digesting and that gas was being wasted. Res could clear the foam from the pits by lighting a match to it. It burnt quickly, like tissue paper. When the farmers came for their fertilizer they came with baskets, expecting to load up on solids. They went home empty-handed and didn't come again. They couldn't carry watery slurry in their baskets.

* * * * *

In the crowded hills of Nepal, Res Fritschy felt alone. He had assumed that he would clean up the technical problems of the biogas plant within four months, at which time the whole system would be turned over to the DDC, which expected a turnkey operation. But Fritschy instead found himself signing on for one four-month contract after another. Every month he would return to Kathmandu for a few days, but he didn't find the solution to the system's problems in town. Resolution renewed, he would return to Pauwa. There, faced with the tiny, insistent, interminable, insoluble problems, he would again begin to despair.

The villagers were hospitable to Res in their own way, bringing him eggs when they had a few extra, or insisting he stop in for tea when he rested on the six-hour climb up to Pauwa from the main trail along the river. But Fritschy would chafe at the time-consuming ceremoniousness, never fully realizing his obligations as a receiver as well as purveyor of gifts. Even though there was room and running hot water in the apartments above the dairy, he lived below in the nursery building—the reforestation funds had been cut upon Rust's departure, and Fritschy said he preferred his privacy. He never mastered the Nepali language, never expecting to stay longer than four more months, so he spoke to the local people in the vocabulary of a child. His tone was unfailingly impatient and reproving, and this made people who had liked Beda Rust shy away from Fritschy. When difficulties arose they spoke to one another, but never to him. He often wished he would fall sick so he could go home.

* * * * *

Fritschy never even built up a friendship with Gyaljen Sherpa, the Nepali cheesemaker who replaced Beda Rust, even though Gyaljen spoke English, French, Nepali, and Sherpa (in their effort to make Pauwa the best cheesery in Nepal, SATA had sponsored his training in Switzerland). Gyaljen had arrived in Pauwa just a few weeks before Fritschy, two weeks after having spent two years in Switzerland. He stayed after Fritschy left, and felt like an exile. Where he grew up, everyone had been a relative, and now he lived amid strangers; he was lonelier than he had been in Switzerland. He says that in the high country all the people had very good hearts, but in Pauwa they bicker and talk behind one another's backs. In Nepal a man who travels from home into the world is called a man who has eaten the wind. Gyaljen had eaten the wind.

Gyaljen did identify the cheesery's problem: if milk is pasteurized at a temperature high enough to kill all the bacteria, it will not then react with the rennet to separate and make cheese.

Cleanliness was still the only solution, but the water system installed by Rust had broken down. The local people, who felt the tap was too far away to walk to, had interfered with the pipes, slashing them at convenient intervals and covering the slashes with loose stones. When Gyaljen wrote to his superiors in the DDC to ask for help, the DDC wrote back to advise him that the people should sterilize their buckets daily with boiling water and whitewash their animals' stalls. Gyaljen, who knew that many of the farmers cut the milk they sold to him with polluted stream water, shrugged.

The reforestation effort started by Beda Rust was turned over to the local people, specifically to the village headman's nephew, Raj Bhadur. He grew tree seedlings and sold them to the villagers for two rupees each, but it wasn't long before he began supplying only fruit trees to be planted beside houses, not on barren hillsides. He found that no one bought fodder or pine trees, and neither did he plant them himself. The tree plantation was still there, and Raj Bhadur even knew of people who had been fined for cutting wood there, but like the other villagers he saw nothing wrong with sending his cows and goats to forage in the protected forest. Everyone did it, and always had. That was the reason the forest had been lost in the first place.

The shortage of fodder limited the amount of milk the cheesery received, and it never reached its projected level. Initial estimates had been as high as 1,000 quarts a day, perhaps because the surveys were done with people like Raj Bhadur and his uncle, who were quite eager to appear prosperous. Often only 400 quarts came in, partly because of the fodder shortage and partly, according to Gyaljen, because of the number of buffalo sold to pay off the loans farmers took out to buy the buffalo.

Once, when Fritschy returned to Pauwa after a couple of weeks in Kathmandu, the biogas digesters had gone haywire. The technician, whom Fritschy had been training for six months, had taken an unscheduled holiday and had dumped all the slurry in one of the three tanks before he left. He thought no one would notice, but all three tanks had stopped digesting—the empty ones because they lost their airtight seal and the full one because it had overflowed.

On the same day, only 192 quarts of milk arrived at the cheesery. Gyaljen explained to Fritschy that the farmers had organized a strike. The price of *ghee* had risen, and farmers were making more money selling *ghee* to the traders, as they had before the dairy had been built. The reason for the increase in the price of *ghee* was huge floods on the Indian plain around the Ganges and its tributaries: many buffalo had been killed, and the ensuing drought had wiped out the fodder for those that remained. The flooding itself was attributed to the destruction of mountain watersheds in places like Pauwa.

Gyaljen had told the farmers that the DDC wouldn't give them more money for their milk, because of the losses already incurred in Pauwa—the place had lost 300,000 rupees in a single year. He had told them that the price of *ghee* stays high for only a few months, while the cheesery pays throughout the year. Without milk, the factory would have to close, he had warned.

The 192 quarts of milk made two big cheeses, weighing about 22 kilos each. The dairymen filled buckets with the leftover whey and poured it into a pipe that debouched at the piggery. Moments later, the sound of screeching pigs began in earnest. In the piggery a sow was dead, her piglets shivering against her stiff body. Another sow stood on her body in order to reach the fresh whey. The piglets' mother had died of fever after giving birth. She wasn't supposed to be breeding, but an uncastrated pig had leaped over a collapsed retaining wall.

All the adult pigs were too fat, but their 120-rupee price tags put them beyond the reach of the villagers so they lived on in the piggery, plaguing Fritschy. To get the biogas the cheesery required, he would need twice as many pigs, but there was not enough food for them in the area. Fritschy's problem was what to do with the pigs. Noble pigs they were, but they were unable to walk Nepal's steep trails, and since they were much too heavy for a man to carry there was no way to get them out. Fritschy considered slaughtering them all and making sausages—but smoking sausages, of course, takes firewood.

* * * * *

"The project sounded so simple," says Fritschy. "Just take pigs, feed them whey and make the cheese. The DDC thought this would be a prestige project. Now they know we can't do it. We will never finish this place." Fritschy finally left Nepal two years after he came, without having solved the problem he had come to solve. No SATA technicians were sent in to replace him. The cheesery was handed over to the DDC, which was to make the final decision as to what to do with the pigs and the biogas plant. Until further notice, the boilers are heated with kerosene.

CHAPTER FIVE

Shade for the Axeman

IN Nepal's middle hills, the steep Himalayan foothills that anywhere else in the world would be called mountains, the 9 million hill farmers aren't to blame for the constant landslides. Were there no people at all in this Himalayan kingdom, the land would still be prone to move. In this rugged terrain between the snowpeaks and the plains, the hills are still adjusting in the aftermath of the greatest collision the world has ever known.

Seventy million years ago India was an immense island that trundled northward toward the great Eurasian continent. The rock that is now the Himalaya, the land that is now Nepal, was hidden deep beneath the sea. As India drew northward, riding on a piece of the earth's crust that furled beneath Eurasia as it hauled India along, the sea narrowed and finally disappeared when, 40 million years ago, India ran aground on the essentially unmoving Eurasian continent.

The tremendous impact of the continental collision cracked India's continental shelf along its margin. The forward slice of India stalled and was eventually pushed up and back over India's plain. Now that slice is the Himalaya, the highest mountain range in the world, still riding aloft on the now-buried front section of the Indian subcontinent. India to this day continues to plough into Eurasia. Like waves around the prow of a ship, the Himalaya clusters at India's margin, raised up by India's ageless and persistent intrusion.

The pressures have cracked and overthrust pieces of the Indian subcontinent three times at the junction, and Nepal encompasses all of them. In the Himalaya, the moving plate's profound force is still being faithfully transformed into vertical lift at an as yet unmeasured rate. The foothills of the giant Himalaya are the rubble of the great collisions. Bordering on the foothills is the Mahabharat Lekh, a ridge to the south, the remains of a second overthrust that began 20 million years ago. Between the Mahabharat Lekh and the flat griddle of India's plain is a third ridge, the Siwaliks, the last and smallest sliver of Indian crust to crack free and overthrust into relief.

These are youthful mountains, and they are still growing. But as they rise they are pounded and polished. In the middle hills, as much as ten vertical miles of overburden have been removed by the storms that ride in from the south and try, unsuccessfully, to vault over them.

Each spring the sun's heat draws moisture from the equatorial Bay of Bengal, to the southeast of India. But while the globe inclines its northern hemisphere toward the sun, the pattern of atmospheric winds, like a loose skin around the planet, struggles to maintain its sunward attitude. The bands of prevailing easterlies near the equator shift northward. Above the Bay of Bengal, where the winter winds blow from the northeast, the southeasterlies begin to dominate.

The monsoon is the result of an altered wind pattern over the whole of South Asia, a pattern that seeks to distribute heat more evenly between land and sea. When spring brings new warmth to the high Tibetan plateau, this massive 12,000-foot desert heats quickly. Then the air above it rises and the southeasterlies that originated over the Bay of Bengal begin to curve toward the central Asian desert, as if to fill the vacuum left by the rising hot air. A huge anticyclonic system develops, an atmospheric pump that drives hot, moisture-laden air from the sea toward the mountains.

When the monsoonal winds reach Nepal they rise and drop their moisture load heavily and quickly before the scarp. A

Nepali monsoon storm has the force and density of a vertical river. It's not uncommon for ten inches of rain to fall in a single day, and rainstorms prevail from the end of May into September. The rain fills the rivers until they undercut their banks. Landslides proliferate. Rivulets cut chasms into the slopes. When the storms abate the rivers lose their force, and the load of sediment, gravel, and boulders they carry at their height is dropped midstream. The rivers then flow higher in their valleys, and the new embankments offer fresh faces for undercutting. The steep hillsides require protection from the rain's onslaught, but the waterlogged farming terraces and treeshorn slopes of Nepal offer little.

The drainage patterns of Nepal's middle hills are elaborately trellised. Flowing water has furrowed the land. The steep-sided hills of middle Nepal are passive receptors of the monsoon's force. All that deflects the rain's downward momentum is a layer of roots and a crown of greenery. Without trees, the bare soil of the hills is loosened by the rains. With nothing to dissipate the rain's force, the waterlogged earth yields suddenly to gravity and the land rushes downhill in a sudden orgy of kinesis.

Everything in these steep hills of the middle Himalaya would slip down toward the nearest river if it weren't tacked down. Sometimes the soil from the outward-sloping terraces, where people grow corn, wheat, and millet, slides off the hills in sheets. More spectacular are the rock fall and soil creep, hill slump and mud flow, all encouraged by the incessant pressure of gravity, all on the precipitous edge of letting go. Land that is bare is the first to move. On treeless mountainsides, the number of landslides doubles. In the middle hills of Nepal, the scantily vegetated community woodlots and pastures lose over twice as much topsoil every year as the full-crowned forests. Where gullying has begun, the erosion rate is 28 times normal.

Loss of soil, loss of land, loss of labor, loss of life—these are considered unavoidable catastrophes in much of the Himalaya, and although they fear them, people have not been able to help themselves. But in Sindhu Polchok, a mountainous district in Nepal, a change has begun. Forest area there is increasing, rather than decreasing. The catalyst for this astonishing turnaround was a young Divisional Forestry Officer (DFO), Tej Bahadur Singh Mahat.

* * * * *

In 1973, the Department of Forestry, a part of Nepal's Ministry of Forestry, transferred Mahat to a new office in Chautara, the district capital of Sindhu Polchok. Mahat had served his first three years with the department at a posting in the heavily forested *terai,* the flat jungle territory beyond the foothills near the India-Nepal border. There he traveled by road, footpath, and elephant to inspect the jungles under his care, and to protect them from encroachers stealing timber or clearing forests for farmland. As DFO, Mahat had the powers of judge and jury over offenders, and he was known in his district as an unflinchingly severe and unbribable official.

Mahat was himself a hillman. He had grown up in the middle mountains of west central Nepal. His first ambition had been to become a fighter pilot in the Indian army, following the tradition of the many men in his large family who had been soldiers with the famous Gurkha regiment in the British army. The idea had sent his mother into a panic, so the disappointed Mahat had studied general science, settled for an outdoor life with plenty of chances for hunting, and gone into forestry.

Mahat rode out from the plains into the mountains of his new posting on a crowded minibus whose horn bleated hysterically at every blind curve on the snaky road. The first thing he noticed about his new assignment was its instability: from his window on the left side of the bus, he counted eighty-six places along the road where the land had slipped down to crash all over the highway. In the hills, the forest under his care had been scavenged down to tussock and stump. Farming terraces had been carved out of government forestland—in one place within spying distance of his new office in Chautara. In some locations the property he had been assigned to oversee had recently taken an abrupt slide into the nearest ravine. "I thought it was a grave situation," he reported later. "I thought something should be done."

Chautara means "resting place" in Nepali. The village, which lies in the east of Nepal, between Kathmandu and the giant mountains, used to be a regular stop on the trading trail between Lhasa and Kathmandu. Now goods and people travel by road, and Chautara retains the diminished prestige of a local headquarters. The village is spread out along part of a long ridge that in the south dips into the Sun Kosi River and in the north merges with the stone and snow mountains above the trees. Chautara's main and only village road covers about a mile of the ridge's long crestline, and the stone houses that line the road on either side expose their backs to the upslope breezes.

The district that Chautara oversees is diverse, even for Nepal. In the district's high north, migratory herdspeople move up- and downslope in counterpoint with the seasonal snow. In the steamy low valleys of these accordion mountains Hindu farmers sweat in their rice fields. What the people have in common is a love of their mountains, for Sindhu Polchok is entirely mountainous. "The air is sweeter here than it is in the terai," they explain. "Food has a better flavor here in the hills." They also share a filial reverence for their king, Birendra Bir Bikram Shah Dev, and an equally strong distrust of officials like Mahat, who suddenly descend on them to administer His Majesty's government.

Several hundred years ago the district below the snowline was almost entirely covered by forest. Chautara offers a bird's-eye view of how things have changed. From the sharply creased valley bottoms to the parallel ridges, farming terraces climb upward like carpeted stairways. Freestanding hills are layered like wedding cakes. On these tiered hills are the tame trees that grow where the farmers allow them, where their shade won't stunt a ripening grain field. Here and there an occasional wild grove colonizes a gully, or a copse grows bravely on untillable landslide slopes. From Chautara's ridge on down to the river, there's no more forest.

Above Chautara, toward the north, the ridgelines lift. These once tree-covered slopes are sunburned pastures now, dull red and hard as brick. Here and there, landslides have exposed clean and glinting bedrock. Only in the far distance are the mountains blue with trees. Above these piney mountains, hanging like storm clouds, are the snowskirted mountains—Shisha Pangma, Langtang, and Dorje Lakpa. Viewed from the sticky paddy fields, these mountains seem to belong to another world.

It's a landscape of sharp pleats, so steep as to make a flatland farmer turn in his plow. Yet Nepali farmers and their armies of ancestors have imposed on the middle mountains a newer geometry. They have restructured the hills. They've created flat farmland in rising layers. There are tiers of wet rice paddies shining like cloud-filled mirrors, and dry corn and millet terraces stepping upward toward the sky. From the river to the ridges, all but the most precipitous slopes have been spaded until the mountains resemble pyramids of tiny right angles. The farmers of these hills have produced one of the most monumental, and one of the most underrated, feats of human engineering in the world. But to turn the mountains into farms, they sacrificed their forests.

In the Himalaya, people and animals have tripped a delicate equation. When people were fewer—fifty years ago, the population of Nepal was only a third of its present 16 million—tradition gave each man, woman, and child the right to take from the forest a head-load of deadwood and a head-load of animal fodder each day. Now on many mountainsides the deadwood has been gleaned, overgrazing has destroyed much of the grass, and the once endless forests have been terraced for farming. Once-wooded slopes are trellised by gullies and stripped of soil by sheet erosion. As if in return for human plundering of the mountains, each year villages disappear beneath landslides.

The forest common lands are the larder of the hill farmers. The poorer the farmers, the greater their need for the commons. It's only on unclaimed land that anything is free: wood for burning, leaves and grasses for animal feed and green manure, honey and herbs for food and medicine. Year in and year out the number of people in the hills grows, their poverty increases, and the forest larder shrinks. The pine-spiked mountains in the far distance below the peaks tantalize. They are a three-day walking journey from Chautara. For the tree-hungry people of the valley farms, these trees might as well not exist.

The modest local woodlands of the lower mountains seem to have been eaten up. The forests have been colonized and hewn into terraces. They've been overgrazed, clear-cut, and eroded down to slippery clay. The trees are gone but the need remains.

In parts of Sindhu Polchok, as in much of Nepal and the Indian Himalaya, the search for firewood takes women miles from their homes: to obtain a full load of wood they must rise before dawn, and they don't return until after dark. In the winter, when fires are needed for heating as well as cooking, some women put in an exhausting two days a week at this job. They're forced to neglect their children. When trees are scarce, cows and buffalo go on short rations. They give less milk and sicken more easily. There's less manure for the fields and harvests fall off. Springs dry up on treeless hillsides; only dirty creekwater is available. Three children in ten die before they're five years old, many of them victims of the dehydration that comes of diarrhea.

By the time Mahat came to Chautara, it was apparent to everyone in Nepal that no social or technological miracle was going to release the hill farmers from their poverty. Huge government ministries and scores of foreign advisors had all been drawn to their aid. In Chautara, Australian foresters were experimenting with fast-growing eucalyptus species, hoping to provide a Band-Aid for the forests' ills. Progress in forestry, public health, education, transportation, and other fields in Nepal was sure but painfully slow. Still, in the middle mountains people were losing ground faster than they were advancing. Progress would surely come with time, but the disappearance of the forests was undermining the hillpeople's ability to survive even until then.

* * * * *

As DFO, Mahat's assignment was to protect the government's forests. For a young man with a family back in the capital, Sindhu Polchok was a better posting than others in the hills, because it was easier to reach from Kathmandu. It was also easier to navigate within this district than in many others. Five roads had been built in its 1 million acres, and that was five more roads than in many districts. But even so, some villages in the steep and rugged territory still lay three and four day's walk from Chautara. Communications traveled no faster: messages were delivered by post, and the postman walked.

"What to do, that was the problem," said Mahat. He had a vast responsibility. He was responsible for the care of forests he couldn't identify. The Ministry of Forestry had yet to draw maps of its own territory.

Some government forest was easy to find. In the terai, for example, Mahat had experienced little difficulty staking boundaries in the tall-tree jungle under his care. The mountains between Chautara and the snow, too, hold forests that are unquestionably the government's, although the perimeters of these forests are often disputed by local people. These highest and lowest forests are valuable to the government for commercial reasons. But it wasn't only the commercially lucrative forest that needed Mahat's protection.

In Sindhu Polchok, the government's lands ran patchily, seemingly at random. Checking with local people, Mahat found himself responsible for a small copse of tropical trees overhanging a river, as well as a ridgetop pine grove another day's walk uphill. He found that when he was out of sight, these groves were no-man's-land.

All these trees had become the property of the government in 1957, when the country was just emerging from a century of closed borders and medieval despotism. The King established many reforms when he gained power in 1951, only to find that the country's treasure was bare. The appropriation of the forests for commercial purposes was one of many strategies devised in order to improve Nepal's finances and introduce the country to the twentieth century.

In retrospect, the law that nationalized the forests was carelessly drawn. The government had desired the timber, but it also had claimed the village common lands—the forestland that for centuries had belonged by custom to the people of Nepal's thousands of mountain villages. To the villagers these common lands are as essential as the air they breathe. By the time the destructiveness of this law became clear, the nation was seemingly unable to reverse the damage.

The government eventually sorted out the problem. When the villagers lost their perceived ownership of their pastures and woodlots, they felt they had also relinquished the responsibility to maintain them. As a result, by the time it reached the ears of the unschooled mountain people, the law had become an excuse to pilfer. By the 1970s many people had farmed forestlands, hurrying before the forestry officer had arrived to mark their boundaries. Much forestland had been picked over. Instead of holding woodlands as a community trust, everyone was scavenging fruits, grasses, leaves, and trees before their neighbors beat them to it. The petty thievery has thinned the forests that remain, and in places woodland has been reduced to barrens. In other spots the remaining trees have been systematically mutilated by people gathering leaves for animal fodder. Formerly fully crowned trees have been pruned until only the tallest trunks carry leaves, and those grow in strangled tufts. Near the villages are battalions of these crippled survivors.

All this, in Mahat's book of operations, was known as encroachment, and it was his job to stop it. Initially he was determined to keep encroachers out of the forest. Fortunately, he failed. His mission was impossible; everyone was a culprit. If he were to arrest all the people who were plundering the government's forests, he would have had to nab the whole district. The Department of Forestry's book of rules and regulations had no solutions to offer. At this point Mahat had to pause, as did most DFOs in these tiny boondocks when they realized the situation. The DFO's duty, it seemed, was to keep persons he couldn't locate from taking wood from forests he couldn't identify.

The DFOs are a varied group, although they're all better educated than the majority of Nepali people. Their jobs are salaried and secure, and the position has some importance in the districts. Yet manning an isolated outpost of the Ministry of Forestry's labyrinthine bureaucracy with an impossible task before them was sometimes too much for the officers. Some DFOs turned their posts into fiefdoms, and cultivated favor-selling as a profitable business. Others concentrated only on the most flagrant abuses of forest law, and left the average village people alone. Some conservative DFOs merely kept their seats warm.

For the most part the DFOs were swaddled in a system that teaches that the realm of response is finite. Once you have learned what is in the book, they were taught, you too know all the answers, and there is no more to learn. The system is one that discourages innovation, and Mahat probably wasn't thinking of innovating when he stepped off the track. He was just tired of sitting in Chautara, waiting for the answers to come to him.

Mahat had gone into forestry because of his love of the outdoor life. He was known as the only DFO in the entire Ministry of Forestry who actually *liked* to walk in the mountains. So he locked his door and went to explore his district. He decided to meet these encroachers face to face and, where he could, talk them out of it. Mahat walked through rice paddies whiskered in green. He climbed and descended centuries-old pathways paved with slate. He edged through gullies that were alive with the polytonal flow of water and rank with the smell of human urine. Everywhere, he stopped to talk. Once they learned that he had come neither to arrest nor to belabor them, the people offered him their habitual, graceful hospitality.

Mahat really was interested. He sat on rugs and on bamboo mats and drank gallons of tea while his hosts agreed with him that yes, it's terrible the way the people encroach on the forest. In fact, they themselves had more than once seen their fellow villagers doing it! It was a shame the way trees were cut and fires were set, and this should indeed be stopped. As conversation warmed, people confided to Mahat that actually, they'd like to stop, but they couldn't.

More than the nation's laws had changed since the 1950s: the population of the country had increased until 13.5 million people were farming in a country only about the size of Tennessee. Today the average hill Nepali lives from the produce of just over a quarter of an acre of cropland, and if present trends continue, that tiny amount will be reduced by a third within twenty years.

For decades there have been places in Nepal where the sheer numbers of people have eaten away the forest. In 1954, Ernest Robbe, a United Nations advisor to Nepal, warned the government that the country was already skating close to disaster.

"Deforestation is the rule, particularly in heavily populated areas where more cropland, grazing land, lumber, and fuelwood are needed," he reported. "Such deforestation frequently assumes disastrous proportions; the shortage of timber results in the use of manure for fuel, so that the unmanured land becomes impoverished, yields shrink, and erosion reduces the cultivable area. All this forms a vicious circle that appears difficult to break without a radical change in such practices." Mahat's new friends explained to him that this was the situation in the lower altitudes of Sindhu Polchok. Further, the population pressure in the hills is not just one of people, they explained, but one of animals as well.

Even more farm animals than people live in the hills. Millions of cows, bulls, and buffalo live in the middle mountains, to provide milk and meat, to pull the plows, and for religious practices. But their most important function is to make manure. Without animal composters there is no fertilizer. In a country with little cash for chemical fertilizer and few roads to deliver it, there is no choice. When farmers are short of manure they leave fields untilled, because they know that the harvest will be too poor to bother with.

Many animals, cows and goats in particular, feed by foraging. They roam through the forests trampling seedlings and gnawing on shoots. Under sharp animal hooves, hillside soil compacts. Where animals graze the only trees standing are tall, mature trees, because none can grow up to replace them. Stripped and overcut as these hills are, the trees would return if the land was protected until new trees became established. If any single act could bring back the forests, it would be keeping animals out of them. When Mahat suggested this to people he met on his walks, they explained the hardships this would cause. Where would they get their firewood and animal fodder if they were barred from the forestland? To many people, it seemed that their government was requesting suicide.

Mahat knew that his ministry hadn't solved the problem. Foresters working for the government had planted hectares of trees, but found that half their reforestation money had to be spent on barbed wire fencing to keep the animals out. Without the active participation of the local villagers, no reforestation scheme had a chance of succeeding, because the people's need for fodder and firewood brought them through and over the fences.

An American Peace Corps volunteer once found a woman within an enclosed forest area lopping trees and cutting grasses. "You must not be here," he warned her. "This is a forest that will be for your children." When he returned the next day, the same woman was standing outside the enclosure. There behind the fence, chopping branches and scything grass, were her children.

* * * * *

The Ministry of Forestry had been formed in the year following the Forest Nationalization Act of 1957, and it was still guided by its original mandate to harvest and sell Nepal's timber. It wasn't equipped to manage Nepal's smaller forest holdings, nor to increase their productivity. It was pitifully equipped to respond to the situation that, in the mid-1970s, was beginning to gain worldwide attention.

Reports were filtering in from the hills that some people were eating only one meal a day, and that firewood shortages were the reason they could no longer cook twice. Women were walking in large groups to gather wood. They had to wander so far from their home villages, and for so many hours, that lone women were being molested by strangers. In wood-short areas, dried dung that would otherwise have fertilized fields was being used for cookfires. The numbers of casualties from monsoonal flooding seemed to be increasing. One strong piece of evidence pointing to drastically increased deforestation and erosion was the emergency situation of a brand new island in the Bay of

Bengal, at one of the many mouths of the Ganges. This island seemed to certify the recent and alarming losses of soil from the mountains.

Erosion is a natural process that occurs in every mountainous area of the world, but in Nepal much more than natural processes were at work. One study reported that a quarter of Nepal's landslides are due to human interference, and another blamed half the erosion on the same cause. Less dramatic but more pernicious are the widely documented topsoil losses from the overcut, overgrazed forestlands. A comparison of two surveys of the middle mountains indicated that within only ten years a third of the forests had been destroyed. A 1978 World Bank report on Nepal's forests warned that all accessible forests in the hills would be gone within fifteen years.

The major underlying factor is human overuse: too many people need the forests, and will continue to do so. The population is growing rapidly—according to the latest census, at a rate of 2.6 percent per year. The average Nepali woman bears six or seven children. The people generally agree that this is too many, but six or seven is barely enough to work the land and carry on the family name, once childhood illnesses and deaths take their toll. Nepal's hill women are wise farmers, and prefer to err on the side of plenty.

There are no simple ways to take the burden off the forests in the time that seems to be left. Industries would bring people money to spend on fuels besides wood. But most goods move in and out of the hills on the backs of men, women, and animals, and roads are few and expensive to engineer and maintain. Market access won't improve quickly. Nepal doesn't have the oil or minerals that would encourage large industry, and small industries, it seems, all need wood too. Tourists want campfires, weavers must boil their dyes, cheesemakers must boil their milk, and roads bring travelers' constant demands for hot tea. Even hydroelectricity, an attractive alternative to wood, is risky due to the sediment that fills the rivers and the reservoirs. Raising the living standards of people in these remote and isolated mountain villages is difficult, and doing it quickly is impossible, as any development advisor will testify.

The Department of Forestry and its ministry certainly had no hope. Mahat wrote to his superiors suggesting that the local people might be the ones best able to manage the district's forests, but the reply he received was scornful. "They told me that if they, with all their training, were unable to manage the forests, they didn't believe that illiterates would be able to do it," he said.

Although people had found Mahat's gospel illuminating, no one was offering to manage the forest for him. Forest protection involves constant vigilance, and one lazy farmer who loosed his cows or cut greenwood could undermine an entire community's sacrifice. An even more immediate danger was from the ministry: people in the mountains had more than once seen trees disappear without warning under contracts granted by the officials. They were afraid that their labors would be undermined by the ministry itself.

Mahat met many local leaders in his treks through the district. One was Nil Prasad Bhandari, the *pradhan pancha* of Thokarpa. The pradhan pancha is the elected head of a *panchayat,* a politically discrete segment of a district that contains nine wards and perhaps twice as many villages. Thokarpa panchayat's main village sits on a mountain rib within sight of Chautara, and over a day's travel away. The forests there were being looted, but this time not by the local people.

Thokarpa is bordered by the Sun Kosi River, and along this river runs the only motorable highway leading from Kathmandu to the north. The dozens of trucks and buses that roll along this road carry hundreds of tradespeople who make their living selling firewood both in the capital and in other villages and tea shops along the highway. These people look to the riverside forests to supply them. In the years since the road was laid, the forests adjacent to Thokarpa had begun to bald, and people had begun to notice the loss. Outsiders were responsible, and so they felt free to complain. Bhandari passed the word to his new acquaintance, Mahat.

Mahat couldn't catch the thieves, who came at all hours and infiltrated the forest at hundreds of entry points. A panchayat that needed trees, however, certainly should have them. He and Bhandari hit upon a scheme whereby Mahat would help Thokarpa start a tree nursery, and the seedlings it grew would be used to restock the nearby government forestland that lay above the village and far from the road. This mountaintop had served for so many years as a cow pasture that there was not a healthy tree to be seen, and the gullies there had climbed right to the peak.

Mahat's plan had no precedent. DFOs served as policemen, not gardeners, so the Forestry Department's budget made no provision for planting or for nursery building. Mahat was forced to be inventive. His nursery was initially a schoolyard corner, and the seedlings were tended by the children. No recompense was available for the villagers, who had to work harder and range farther for fuel and fodder, nor were wages paid to the people who planted the trees. There were objections in the village, of course. People expected to lose cows due to the diminished pasture, and, in fact, cows were lost as they stumbled from the steeper pastures that remained.

The deaths of a few cows could be rationalized. Cows are sacred in Nepal and can't be slaughtered, but no one mourns when a weak or diseased cow staggers off a mountain. The real objection lay in the people's strong and emotional distrust of government officials, and Mahat's initial severity was still remembered. People weren't about to voluntarily police this new woodland—especially for an officer who didn't hesitate to punish them when they practiced their habitual thinning and pruning.

Mahat won them over with a proposition that should go down in the annals of the Department of Forestry. He used a well-established bureaucratic procedure to reverse departmental policy. He found a legal loophole that returned the responsibility for, and the rewards from, the forest to the people.

Until Mahat's legalistic coup, only the DFO or his designated nominee had the legal power to grant sales of government-owned timber to outside buyers. Usually a DFO nominated one of his colleagues in Kathmandu. It was an acknowledged setup for exchanging political favors. The people out in the villages were the last to discover to whom the trees from the local forest had been awarded. Unless this system were changed, people knew that their trees, a crop of work and sacrifice, could disappear at any time—sold by permission of the DFO or his distant nominee. Mahat's nominee as grantor of these sale permits was Thokarpa panchayat's forestry committee—a committee newly convened, at Mahat's suggestion, specifically for this purpose. Bhandari was a member, as were other leaders and farmers in the panchayat. Essentially, the move returned control of the forests to the people who needed them. It was a reasonable solution and one altogether outside the people's experience with DFOs. They still didn't trust government officers, but now they trusted Mahat.

With the pradhan pancha and all his local muscle guarding the trees, the place almost reforested itself. Within a couple of years the grass on the mountaintop was a third again as plentiful, and the chir pines grew measurably higher every year. The pradhan pancha was able to ease off on his strong policing as it became clear to the local people why they were being kept away. Today the ridge is fleeced with twenty-foot pines, and the people expect to use the local forestry committee to assign tree sales to themselves. They want to use pine resin in a turpentine factory that they hope to bring to the village.

"The immediate value of the forest is for fuel and for the grasses, but in the long future, the people of Thokarpa will be given paying jobs," the assistant pradhan pancha of Thokarpa asserted.

"Yes, at first it caused hardship," agreed a gray-haired village woman, "but now I like this forest. Now I can squat in the shade!"

Mahat had prescribed pine for Thokarpa's commons, although broadleaf trees would have been more immediately useful. The land had been so eroded there that broadleaves wouldn't have survived; chir pine, on the other hand, flourishes on degraded land. Still, pine is a commercial tree, valuable in Thokarpa because Thokarpa is close both to the road and to transportation to city markets. These people envision that a valuable cash crop will be harvested over the years.

Despite his growing familiarity with the district, Mahat made little progress outside of Thokarpa. Finding ways to enlist people in villages far from the road—and this was the majority of them—would take another approach. Then, in 1976, Mahat received a message from Laxman Dong, the pradhan pancha and virtual dictator of a panchayat called Banskarka.

* * * * *

Banskarka, unlike Thokarpa, is two full days' travel from the main road. The panchayat spreads over a mountainside from the Indrawati River up to the ridgetop, and Laxman Dong's home village, Danga Durbar, lies about in the middle. As in Thokarpa, farmers grow rice in the warmer lower reaches of the panchayat near the river, but unlike Thokarpa, Banskarka's 8,000-foot-high upper reaches are forested with stupendous, moss-bearded rhododendron trees. Thokarpa's Nil Prasad

Bhandari, like the majority of Nepalis, is a Hindu, and his ancestors migrated to Nepal northward from India. Banskarka, farther northeast of Chautara and closer to the Tibetan border, has a Tamung majority. Tamungs migrated south from Tibet only a few hundred years ago. Their language is similar to Tibetan, and like Tibetans, they are Buddhist. Laxman Dong is a Tamung.

Laxman Dong, a wealthy and erect man in his sixties, is the scarred veteran of thirty years of panchayat politics. He has a scholarly look because of thick spectacles, which he wears to protect his left eye, which is blind. Dong lost it in an election about fifteen years ago. According to village tale tellers, he was ambushed by some of his political opponents, who knifed him around the eyes and left him for dead. Now Dong's good eye is still bright and watchful. His blind eye incessantly weeps.

In lower Banskarka, where his power is strongest, Dong's position is almost hereditary. His father was the local tax collector under the Rana prime ministers. Dong maintains his dominance in the panchayat by skillfully cultivating the support of the influential lamas who live in the monastery on the ridgetop, hours from Danga Durbar. To think of the lamas as maroon-robed parish priests would be a mistake. They're more like pastors, parents, teachers, family doctors, and union bosses all rolled into one. They have authority over life's events from cradle to cremation, and all seasons in between. Banskarka's Tamungs might argue with their pradhan pancha, but they wouldn't with the lama—or at least not as loudly.

Laxman Dong's influence also comes from his long record of achievement. He is adept at extracting labor from people, and has instilled a local boosterism in his supporters that is unusual in the district. Banskarkans constantly grumble at Dong's heavy-handed enforcement of labor tax, yet they're tremendously proud that their panchayat has water pipes, irrigation canals, a school, a health post, and beautifully maintained flagstone pathways. Although it is far from the wealthiest, Banskarka is the most comfortable and developed panchayat in the Indrawati valley.

When Mahat responded to Dong's invitation, he had two surprises waiting for him. First, Dong had heard of Thokarpa's nursery and wanted to have one in Banskarka, too.

"Laxman Dong only wanted a tree nursery because he did not want Banskarka to fall behind Thokarpa," claimed one Banskarkan. "Dong is very much an admirer of Bhandari." Actually, and this was Mahat's second surprise, intradistrict competition was only the smallest parcel of the truth: Dong loved trees.

When Mahat first visited the panchayat, Banskarka already seemed to have less need of a nursery than did most panchayats in Mahat's care: Mahat was astounded to find that Laxman Dong had been enforcing forest protection in his village for over a decade. Dong's rationale for protecting Banskarka's forests was not to grow commercially valuable pine trees, or to give villagers firewood, but that he felt his religion required it. Dong, a thinking man, had discovered in deforestation a theological dilemma.

Among Tibetan Buddhists, the preferred funeral practice is cremation, although in many places in Tibet only the rich could afford it. Banskarka's Tamungs, too, prefer cremation. Their funerals take place in a small pine grove, not far up the mountain from Dong's house at Danga Durbar. If cremation was not expensive in cash in Banskarka, it was expensive in labor: one funeral requires about ten headloads of wood, or enough to keep a family warm and cooking for over a month.

To perform the funeral, people would gather their wood, choose a small spot on the burning ground and clear it, burn the body, and after the ceremony, gather stones to build a cairn that would be left to mark the spot. Laxman Dong had noticed that the grove contained more and more cairns, and fewer and fewer trees. If the practice continued, Dong's own funeral would be performed on the slope of a cairn-studded desert.

Dong has explained that he was moved to protect the trees because he likes their shade and fruit, and because he believes that trees have health-giving properties. A living hillside of trees appeals to him more than a cemetery of dead stones; perhaps because they live, Dong concluded, they should be protected. This was a discovery, Dong explained later, that took him up the mountain to enlist the help of the lamas. "Buddhists don't kill," he remembered telling them. "Life is what grows. When you take the life of a tree, is it not a life?" The monks had to agree.

Theirs is a ritual-soaked society, but in many ways a pragmatic one. The Tamungs don't kill for meat, but neither are they vegetarians. They eat meat that has been slaughtered for them by a special caste of butchers. Therefore Dong and the monks determined that the cremation ceremonies could proceed, as long as the people gathered only fallen and dead wood. The question was where to find it. There was none left in the pine grove. The closest broadleaf forest to the village was along the steep river gorge and it, too, was grossly picked over.

In Laxman Dong's youth there had been far fewer people in Banskarka. There had been enough land so that people could burn over a forested patch, use it for a few years, and then let it go fallow. The forests had never failed to recover in those fields. He knew that if this riverside jungle were allowed to rest, in a few years there would be plenty of deadwood.

Dong spoke about his ideas to the Banskarkans. He quoted Buddha: "The forest affords protection to all beings, offering shade even to the axeman who destroys it." Yet despite his considerable powers of oratory and lama-backed spiritual coercion, people were slow to accept this new idea. So he devised what some of the gulled villagers believe, in retrospect, to have been a very clever trick. With promises of food and beer, he lured all the villagers to a ban bhoz, a giant picnic, literally a feast in the forest. Once they had been baited and snagged, he harangued them until all the men had signed a piece of paper pledging themselves to their pradhan pancha's new forest protection scheme.

For illiterate people, a written and signed promise is broken at risk of certain, although unspecified, punishment. Loudly complaining, the men nevertheless formed a corps of guards who watched the forest day and night, without pay. The women in the fifteen families closest to the forest bore the brunt of the scheme. They lost their foraging ground, and continued to object to the protection scheme. The men, however, began to enjoy themselves.

Days are seamless in the villages, marked by repetitive sequences of family events, religious rituals, and discussions over the price of rice. The protected forest was exciting news. It soon.became the richest foraging grounds in the area. Scaring away people from the neighboring villages gave the young guards something useful to do. They had become village vigilantes and they all felt like heroes. According to one guard, "It was the beginning, and we were the foundation."

"The people from the next village had no forest," Dong recalled. "They had no choice. They had to come here. Each day they would come, and the guards would catch them and seize their scythes and baskets. The other villagers needed this forest so much that they would say, that is all right. We will bring others tomorrow. On the next day, the second scythe and basket would be taken. This was happening every day, and still the people did not stop coming into the forest. Soon these people learned that we in Banskarka had sold their baskets and their scythes and made a large feast with the money. After that, they, too, began to stop people from coming into their forest."

Today a walk up the Indrawati River shows the results. The closer to Danga Durbar, the larger the trees and the thicker the undergrowth, as if the care of the forest were rippling outward from a stone thrown by Laxman Dong.

Perhaps most important was the idea that fixed itself in the minds of Banskarka's younger generation of farmers, who had never seen Banskarka in the days of slash-and-burn agriculture. Suddenly the forest was not a fast-emptying larder. Trees had been transfigured to become a crop that could be planted, nurtured, and grown. "After three years of protection the face of the forest was different," reported Krishna Bahadur, one of the first forest guards. "We had not realized that the forest could be grown up this way."

Perhaps more important to Laxman Dong, his own status in Banskarka was reconfirmed. Among Danga Durbar's Tamungs, anyway, his new ideas now went unquestioned. As Krishna Bahadur said, "If there is a mouth, you do not drink water from the nose. The leader is here to make decisions. Why should I?"

"When someone dies the family members want to make the departed soul happy and they do not care about the cost. They will do anything," said Dong. "I told the people, since you want your departed to be happy, if you plant a fruit tree, many people will enjoy fruit and shade. The more comfortable are the people here, the happier is the soul. And when a child is born, where is it born? In a heated room, and the heat comes from the forest. From birth to death, you need the forest.

"At the name-giving ceremony we say, May you live long. Now we say in Banskarka, May you live long like the tree, and may you provide for people as the tree does. I have found that people who believe this will plant trees when a son is named, and look after the trees like their own children. After death the tree is still there, and if it flourishes it is better salvation."

He added confidentially, "For each and every change, you have to color it with religion."

"It was fate that put Mr. Mahat in the same district with Laxman Dong," reflected Pashupati S.J.B. Rana, a former representative from Sindhu Polchok to the national parliament in Kathmandu. "Banskarka is extremely unusual. It is the only village in the district where 80 or 90 percent of the development is done by the people themselves, with no help from the government."

In late 1976, Rana, who was then minister of education, landed in Banskarka. He came in a helicopter that landed on a flat helipad that people had carved out of the mountainside above the nursery that very morning. A work crew had been awake since before dawn clearing and leveling an area for the helicopter to land. No one there had seen a helicopter before, so no one knew what to expect. The Banskarkans managed to level a pad about the size of a baseball diamond in about eight hours.

Rana and his companion, the minister of agriculture, dropped out of the sky like gods, an effect which had not been underestimated by Laxman Dong, who had stage-managed the affair. The machine disgorged the politicians and everyone pressed palms together in respectful greeting. Laxman Dong made a welcoming speech. The occasion was the dedication of the tree nursery, the first in the country to be built on village land by village people—because Mahat had not been able to grant Dong's request, Banskarka had done it alone.

* * * * *

The success of Thokarpa notwithstanding, Mahat had not been able to convince his department that a nursery devoted to fruit and fodder trees—those most valuable to forest encroachers but next to useless as timber—fit within departmental policy. Mahat had then appealed to the Nepal-Australia Forestry Project (NAFP), whose field headquarters for testing nonnative fast-growing trees was located in Chautara. Although they couldn't support the nursery, the NAFP was happy to send a trained Nepali nurseryman to Banskarka, and to pay his wages as well. The Australians soon followed up with a proposal to the government to finance a development program to encourage village nurseries throughout the district. The Australian theory was that the combination of an enthusiastic DFO, opportunity, and local incentive might be the basis for a more broadly based reforestation scheme.

Weeks before the nursery dedication at Banskarka, the pradhan pancha's labor taxes had spaded out terraces from the funeral ground. Overlooking the terraces where the seedlings would sprout, a nursery building to house the tools and nurseryman and his assistants rose from the plentiful supply of rocks in the pine grove. Dong had ordered all the small cairns to be dismantled in order to construct the nursery. Scarlet bougainvillaea was trained over the doorway. The building was welcoming, clean, watertight and, for a long time, empty. No one dared to sleep there. Not until Mahat himself spent a few nights in the new building were the nurseryman and his young assistants convinced that the stones didn't hold the disgruntled spirits of their dead relatives.

These extraordinary efforts, and the unusual alliance of the Australians with the DFO, had not been lost on Laxman Dong. "It is like moths to the light," he told the crowd on dedication day. "When you do something for progress, the visitors come to see. You think that people outside this panchayat do not know what we do here, but they know. These distinguished gentlemen have come to Banskarka, and this is your reward."

The visiting ministers explored the nursery and the new crematorium. The path to the pine grove was bordered with newly planted trees. There were nearly completed irrigation canals that had taken years to install and had more than doubled crop production. The men visited the water taps and noticed, but did not visit, the freshly dug privies. Tea was served in china cups brought from the pradhan pancha's own kitchen. Then the two ministers climbed into the helicopter and flew back to Kathmandu. The agriculture minister had been so impressed that he had left behind 5,000 rupees so Banskarka could finish its last irrigation canal.

The village women wandered off to find firewood and to cook the evening meal, and the men retired to the nursery building for more tea and a discussion of the day. Today, they're still talking about it.

Little has changed in Banskarka since then. Laxman Dong still rules. The broadleaf jungle is no longer patrolled by gangs of volunteers. Now each family is taxed three baskets of grain a year to maintain a permanent forest watchman and his family. "Now my grain feeds the forest," noted Krishna Bahadur.

Bahadur's fields are near this forest. Now he complains about leopards that disturb his chickens. A couple of years ago a hyena loped through Danga Durbar, the first hyena anyone had seen in years. Some people say they're afraid to go outside at night, although on a mountainside that hasn't seen jungle like theirs for a couple of decades, this may be a boast.

The nursery building still stands, although its useful life as a nursery is over. Within seven years all of the land within convenient walking distance of the nursery had been reforested. Now the seedlings used for religious ceremonies come from a nursery located further up the mountain, at the request of Dong and the lamas.

Parts of the panchayat have continued to resist the pradhan pancha's doctrine. The territory in the middle of Banskarka panchayat is under the control of Dong's political rivals, and reforestation there has failed. His opponents have accused Dong of withholding nursery services from them. Dong counters that the people of middle Banskarka lose their plantations because they are not as motivated to protect them as are the people of Danga Durbar.

Dong maintains control of forestry in Banskarka. He, his youngest son, and their appointees still make up a panchayat forestry committee that, like Thokarpa's, determines who gets permission to cut logs in the forests. Yet Dong's attention has shifted. A few years ago the lamas convinced Dong to campaign for a seat in the national parliament. He was soundly defeated. Now he is aging, and his rivals, headed by a wealthy nephew, are still vigorous.

"We used to hear so much about forests when we visited Laxman Dong," said the former pradhan pancha of a neighboring panchayat. "Now he talks about politics."

The most startling effects of Dong, Mahat, and Bhandari's work are apparent not in Banskarka and Thokarpa, but in other panchayats throughout Nepal. It was proved that unschooled villagers could be excellent foresters, given the right circumstances. Now DFOs and forestry extension workers are trying similar methods throughout the country. For example, within Mahat's old district alone, thirty-six tree nurseries have been built through the NAFP, and requests for half again as many are waiting to be filled. The young DFO in Chautara—he third since Mahat left to continue his education in forestry in Australia—takes for granted his status as combination policeman, gardener, and development manager, a job description that has evolved since Mahat. The NAFP's project is widely acknowledged as one clear development success, among many failures.

By 1977 the government had become uncomfortably aware of the costs of deforestation in the middle mountains of Nepal, and of its own inability to respond. Although it would be impossible to undo the effects of its past forestry policies, the government believed it would be possible to revise them. Advice was sought from Mahat, who returned to the capital in the bleating minibus, where he helped to draft new forestry laws. Legislation was passed in 1978 and revised in 1980, and its design leaned heavily on Mahat's experiences in Sindhu Polchok. Government forests and forest products are now the property of panchayats where people are willing to demonstrate their ability to protect and plant them. Under the law, 40 percent of the national forestland is available to the panchayats.

In addition, the government requested assistance from the United Nations Food and Agriculture Organization and the World Bank. A nationwide Community Forestry Development Project—backed by 40 million dollars from the World Bank—was planned based on the conviction that what had been achieved in Sindhu Polchok could be repeated throughout the country.

By 1984 the Community Forestry Development Project had established 350 community nurseries. More than 7 million seedlings had been planted. Only about 65 percent of the seedlings survived, and according to the director of the national project the people's commitment to caring for their new trees was almost a direct measure of the enthusiasm and backing of the local DFO.

Nepal is far from out of—or into—the woods. According to Nepal development expert Michael Wallace, even if all the proposed planting and protection schemes are carried out successfully, the needs of the growing population will still exceed the abilities of Nepal's forests to provide for them. And however successful the community forestry programs are, they still won't touch the deeply entrenched poverty, illiteracy, and overcrowding in the country. Landslides continue to threaten homes and villages, and terraces still lose fertile soil seasonally to the rains. But there has been some change.

In the Chautara district jail live two inmates, a man and a woman. Both are serving life sentences. The woman is guilty of the murder of her lover's wife. The man's crime was felling a tree in a protected forest. This may say something about the value of human life in Chautara, or it may say something about the value of trees.

CHAPTER SIX

Helena's Epiphany

IT takes some effort to get to Ladakh. One way takes a pony and yak trail northeast from India's Punjab plain across the 17,000-foot passes of the westernmost tail of the Himalaya. One branch of this route passes through Hemis, a Tibetan Buddhist monastery in central Ladakh where, according to legend, Jesus Christ spent his lost years. There is a paved road. This route takes two days, driving from Srinigar, the capital of Kashmir, across 12,000-foot passes, but the road is blocked by snow and avalanche for seven months of the year. From the north there are the old caravan routes from Yarkand and Turkestan, and from Tibet in the east a route from Lhasa—when the Chinese army tried these in 1962 they found half the Indian army arrayed on the passes against them. Or an airplane arrives, two days a week, from New Delhi.

To those fainthearts who choose to come to this northerly district of India by plane, arrival in Ladakh is a shock to the system. The airport is almost 9,000 feet higher than the one in New Delhi, and it's a toss-up whether it's the altitude or the view that takes your breath away and makes your heart pump wildly. Ladakh and its mountains are perched on the high plateau between the western tail of the Himalaya and the eastern snout of the Karakoram. Its main river, which runs in the valley below the airstrip, is the legendary Indus. The valley is wide and rolls gently uphill before gutting itself on steep mountainsides. The surrounding mountains rise in uneven layers of upended sediment. This was once sea floor, and the mountains have the claylike tones of unfired pottery. Across the river valley, the snowy mountains peak at 25,000 feet.

In the center of the valley lies the village of Spituk, its windblown poplars and fields of barley a green oasis in the high desert. At the top of a lone rocky outcrop is the monastery of Spituk, and clinging to the sides like so many barnacles are the whitewashed adobe homes of its monks. To the northeast is the capital city of Leh, another feathery green exclamation in the monotonic valley. Leh has its back to the mountain; another monastery and the old palace, abandoned and crumbling, loom stonefaced above it.

Ladakh is stony mountains and gravel valleys. People heat and cook with dried yak dung. They labor in the fields from dawn until half past dark, and the only man-made sounds are the horns, drums, and bells of the monasteries. Ladakh is a mountain-ringed desert where life hasn't progressed beyond the fifteenth century. If they can handle the altitude, the tourists love the place.

Ladakh was not opened to tourism until 1975, when Indian military interests finally decided that there was no longer any danger from the Chinese. Politically speaking, it has been a territory of India since 1834, but for over a thousand years it has been part of the Tibetan theocracy—it is even known as "little Tibet." There are more than a dozen active, easily accessible monasteries full of art and monks, and the culture still produces both. In Tibet, the Chinese tried to consolidate their power by eradicating Buddhist culture. They destroyed paintings, burned books, and bombarded ancient monasteries during target practice. In Ladakh the culture is intact and abundantly salable to tourists.

A walk in Ladakh can bring out the Brueghel in anyone. Everywhere you look, people are engaged in the simple daily tasks that can be so mysterious to the urban tourist. Ladakhis have lived and flourished here for thousands of years, amid conditions that would kill most Westerners within a week. Only about four inches of rain fall a year, and the snow that falls often sublimes directly from ice to water vapor before it has a chance to melt. In order to live here, people have patiently rechanneled the streams to flow into the stone ditches outlining every barley field and the crops suck life from the icy cold, glacierfed streams that debouch from the sere mountains all around. In other countries, the ground is naturally covered with soil; in Ladakh, a farmer has to manufacture his own.

In the annals of human interference in mountain regions, Ladakh is one of the few true success stories: Ladakhi villagers have actually managed to make something from nothing.

* * * * *

Ngawang Tsering is a short, slender young man. He has a preoccupied air and habitually hums snatches of religious chants to himself. He is the eldest son of a family that makes its home in Nurla, a village where the Indus gorge widens to about half a mile. He received his higher education at Vishva Bharati University, near Calcutta, where he completed a doctorate in Buddhist philosophy. Before 1962, he would have gone to Lhasa for this sort of learning, but the Chinese closed the border and dozens of Ladakhi boys had to come home, some traveling across Tibet by foot with guerilla herdsmen. The monks lost a good candidate in Ngawang Tsering, for he is a devout Buddhist: his faith is the scaffolding of his life. Monks oversaw the death of his father and the marriage of his brother. His family tills the monastery's lands as a sort of tax, and in return is assured of food during times of drought. The monks look at the stars and tell his brother and grandfather when to plow their fields. The system is ancient, feudal, and symbiotic.

The Buddhist philosophy is often summed up as a matter of simple steps, known as the Four Noble Truths: Life is suffering, or dissatisfaction; the cause of suffering is craving, or desire, or attachment to an idea that doesn't match up with the reality; there is a way to escape suffering; it is to follow the Buddha's teaching. It has been said that these truths are the core of the religion, and the rest is detail.

Over the centuries, the details have been illuminated over and over again by Ladakh's religious artists. Buddhist practice is the focus of all of Ladakh's artistic work, in the manner of the medieval Christians. The walls of the monasteries and the individual family shrines are alive with paintings of the *boddhisattvas,* the beings who have escaped from suffering and have elected to stick around to help the rest of us. Their aspects range from benign to demonic, but they are a rare taste of hot color in a land of cinderheap mountains and moonscape valleys. No one in Ladakh can find his way around these paintings in English as well as Ngawang Tsering, and for this reason he is the country's best tourist guide. He itemizes the iconography slowly and patiently. Of what looks like a pair of devils clinging together in a naked embrace—a tourist favorite—he might say, "She is red, because she is devoted to the service of all beings. She is naked because she is free of the veil of passion. He is Appearance and Boundless Compassion, and she is Emptiness. They stand within the fire of supreme wisdom, which destroys all obstacles. They trample on time."

Ngawang Tsering can go on this way for hours, explaining each object grasped by the figures' ten hands, the significance of each color, the placement of each foot. The tourists are impatient, asking a lot of sharp questions he can't answer. They expect their guide's patter to match that of guides in the European cathedrals. But he is unfailingly polite. The tourists do not understand that, aside from the upper strata of lamas and the educated people of Leh, Ladakh is full of people who do not depend on the written word for information. Most Ladakhis can read neither the Hindi that is the official language of India nor the Parsi common in Jammu and Kashmir (the Indian state in which Ladakh is situated) nor the Tibetan of their religious culture, so these paintings, with incredible significance of detail, are the books that teach the people about their own living religion. The Ladakhi word for "painter" means "writer of the gods." In a way, Ngawang Tsering is teaching "illiterate" Westerners to read.

The prophet Modentika said that in this world Ladakh was destined to be a stronghold of Buddhism, a prophecy that time has fulfilled. From an early age Ladakhis learn that all worldly desires are unreal, and that relief from life's sufferings can be found in detachment from these desires. It is an ideal philosophy for a place where life is hard and there's not much to go around, but there is another reason for the richness of Buddhism in Ladakh. Buddha taught in northern India in the fifth century B.C. Two hundred and fifty years later the emperor of India, Ashoka, discovered his teachings. Ashoka was an enthusiastic convert. By general edict, all the country became Buddhist, and he massed his considerable wealth and might behind a gigantic evangelical effort. He recruited monks instead of soldiers and sent them as missionaries to the most remote portions of his universe. Some of them ended up in Ladakh, and this pocket of Ashoka's empire has been Buddhist longer, and with less competition, than any other place on earth.

Ngawang Tsering's family, which he supported on his guide's wages while also paying for his schooling, is suffering from a labor shortage. His father is dead, and his mother, his maternal grandparents, and his younger brothers and sisters have been left to run the farm. The family, while not wealthy, is secure. They live in a large, well-built house: animals on the ground floor, people above. The top floor holds sleeping rooms, a large and sunny courtyard, and the family shrine, where fierce *bodhisattvas* cling to the walls by their paint. It's a Tibetan-style building with whitewashed walls that drift gracefully inward at an

85-degree angle. The windows have bright sashes, painted primarily red, yellow, and blue, like the *boddhisattvas* upstairs, and shutters to close against the cold. The house is spacious and old, built in the tradition of community effort, a showpiece for each local craftsman's work.

On the main floor is a long, low-ceilinged room where smoke from an open fire blackens the beams and the face of Ngawang Tsering's mother before wafting out through a hole cut wishfully above it. The furnishings are sparse: a couple of decorated tea tables, squatter's height; some seat-sized wool rugs. One wall is dimpled with brass and copper pots, the most scrubbed items in the house. Ngawang Tsering's grandfather's carved ivory prayer wheel rests on a battery-powered radio. Everything the family possesses—like the tea churn, where tea, butter, and salt are agitated until they come out a foamy pink—is well made, handcrafted, and passed along for generations.

It is part of the Buddhist philosophy to see reality as it is, to accept change, and not to cultivate sentimental attachments to things as they used to be. That attitude takes on the complexion of household advice for Tsering's mother, a slender, narrow-faced woman in her forties. She is not attached to preserving her household items, but instead eagerly looks for new forms and functions for them. Everything she uses goes through several different incarnations. She keeps the dirty dishwater to feed the animals. Her clothes are worn until they're in tatters, and then they're used to dam leaky irrigation canals. Tin cans, which she seldom acquires, armor poplar saplings from foraging livestock. The barley that ferments to make beer is dried and roasted afterward for eating. Apricot kernels are stone crushed, their nuts are removed, and the tiny nuts are crushed for their oil. The leftover fibrous rape cures the livestock's digestive problems. Trees are never felled; they are pollarded to save enough of the main trunk so that new shoots can grow from it. Animal dung is collected for fuel, and ashes are mixed with more dung to make fertilizer. Nothing is wasted, nothing is saved, nothing is spared, and nothing is lost.

When Ngawang Tsering comes home, he doesn't usually bring gifts. He's not attached to possessions. Books are his greatest temptation, and he keeps his odd collection near his bed. There are abstruse texts on Buddhism and Hinduism—he reads Hindi, Tibetan, and English, and is proficient in all three alphabets—but there is one volume on solar power, printed in the United States. His fifteen-year-old sister is learning to read English, but his books are beyond her, as is her own textbook. It contains sentences like "Anand beat me this morning"—an odd thing to teach a schoolgirl in a country remarkable for its Buddhist-inspired nonviolence.

Their mother has one new possession. She bakes her bread on an asbestos mat. This is a popular innovation introduced by the army: it never burns her hands. She has never heard warnings about the link between asbestos and cancer and would probably have disregarded them if she had. Cancer isn't that common in her village—or if it is, it isn't identified as such. Tuberculosis is widespread, and Ladakhis often have hernias and bad teeth. Eye diseases, like tuberculosis attributable to long months in smoky rooms, are often seen. But the army doctor in Leh reports that the only cancers he sees are cancers of the mouth, the result of poorly fitting false teeth.

Like his father before him, Ngawang Tsering's younger brother runs the farm. Also like their father, the middle brother is an *amche,* a traditional Tibetan herbal doctor. Ngawang Tsering let the traditional options open to him as eldest son devolve to his brother when he decided to become a religious scholar. The middle brother's wife, a sunny girl of seventeen, joined the family only a short time ago. The family had heard of the girl, who is from another village, through relatives. Ngawang Tsering took a bus to her village and watched her from a distance, hard at work in a field. On the basis of that and hearsay, the wedding was arranged.

Traditionally, Ladakhi brothers shared a wife. Polyandry was Ladakh's way of controlling the population. But the national government banned the practice in 1941, and in 1962, with the Chinese armies looming on the borders, the Indian army expanded its garrison in Ladakh. Suddenly, young men who previously could choose either to join a brother's marriage or a monastery were being offered jobs that gave them the means to support their own families. Now polyandry is on its way out; farms are being divided among the children, and the birth rate is increasing, with more women in marriages. Polyandrous marriages have almost entirely vanished in Leh. But this is but one of dozens of changes.

In 1975, only about a hundred tourists came to Ladakh's capital; in 1980, there were over twelve thousand. There were no hotels in 1975; now there are about 150. There were two restaurants; now there are dozens, as well as taxis, trinket shops, beggars from India, flush toilets, and a lot more flies. Leh has sporadic deisel-generated electricity, a radio station, and, in one hotel, central heating.

Twenty buildings in and around Leh display a remarkable example of small-scale development aid, a vindication of the small-is-beautiful principle: passive solar collectors. The locals call them *shel kang,* "glass houses." Most of them were installed by a tourist who came to Leh in 1975 and has come back every year since: Helena Norberg Hodge.

Helena was never an ordinary tourist. In 1975, a German filmmaker invited her to Ladakh as a linguist. She can pick up any language almost as fast as she hears it. When she's exposed to a new language, she seems to absorb it almost involuntarily. When the film crew left, Helena stayed. She found room with the Christian Moravian missionaries, in a mission that has been maintained since the 1850s. By the end of the summer, the

Ladakhis say, her mastery of the language was perfect. She was the first European to learn it in over fifty years. She is a striking woman, much taller than the average Ladakhi woman, and better preserved as well. Despite the blue eyes that reflect her English/Swedish ancestry, her hair is thick and black and swings freely to her waist in the Ladakhi fashion. The people in town began to call her *Atche Helena,* "Big Sister Helena."

By the next summer she knew Leh well enough to see changes begin. As the city adjusted to the new tourist trade, Helena feared that Ladakh was about to enjoy more of the West than it could stand. She tried in her own way to preserve the culture, by writing a Ladakhi-English dictionary and by cautioning the locals against heedless development. Her message: "You just don't know what you're in for." In contrast with a world situation that still panics her, Ladakh seemed nearly perfect.

"There may not be many traditional cultures left that have so much to teach us, but there certainly are a few, and I think Ladakh is the best of them," said Helena. Her tone, which tends to rise as if pitch were a measure of earnestness, was rising. "When I went to Ladakh with the anthropological film team, I found the place wonderful and fascinating, and above all, I found a human population in a society that for at least a thousand years had maintained a very careful ecological balance in an extremely fragile environment.

"In the West, when I talk about the Ladakhi people's happiness, I'm dismissed as a romantic," she continued. "After my second year there I suddenly realized that I, too, had been subconsciously looking for some hidden repression or unhappiness beneath the surface. It was part of my Western upbringing to be convinced that people could not be as happy as these people seemed to be. Perhaps it's their Buddhist culture, but the Ladakhis have a bubbling vitality, something that's far too rare in our society. The happiness of people is something we really have to take into account. You can already see, in the modernized section of Ladakh, that the people are not as happy."

About ten thousand people live in Leh, the only modernized section of the country. This dusty and dung-splattered town is larger by a factor of a hundred than other settlements in the valley. Its buildings are of sun-dried brick, and most of its streets are no wider than a village alley. Only the main street allows two-way traffic. Shops line the main street, and women sit along the curbs selling vegetables. Jeeps and buses and trucks from Kashmir, the road's only destination, raise the stink of diesel fumes. Helena insists that this town, whose air was crystal clear when she first came, now has one of the worst air pollution problems in Asia.

Hundreds of Ladakhis work for a living here, for the army, for the government, and in tourist-related businesses. These institutions have brought that Western invention, the desk job, to Ladakh. Self-sufficiency always used to be enough: villagers would barter their labor for goods, and individual members of communities would help other people in the knowledge that their help would be remembered and rewarded. Now a salary is necessary too.

A money economy brings other things in its wake, like crime and poverty. Theft was previously unheard of in Leh, but now people are starting to put bars on their windows. There was a murder recently, the first in this city in living memory. The young men in town are beginning to want motorbikes and polyester shirts. "These people need to cross the poverty line," says the south Indian economist for Ladakh's Desert Development Agency. "India has decided that any household taking in less than 300 rupees (about $37) per month is in poverty. In the winter the people here do not care to work, and so we are bringing in workers from another part of India. But all this will be changing."

The government's way to calculate poverty is to count the

number of people without a job and call them unemployed. Unfortunately, government statistics take no account of the fact that hardly anyone works in the winter. Ladakh is one of the coldest inhabited places on earth, and during the winter the people essentially hibernate. The temperature hangs at about – 40 degrees, where the Fahrenheit and centigrade scales cross. Heating is a trial, since fuel is scarce. There are no forests, and the only fuel is animal dung that the people spend half the summer gathering and carrying back to their homes. Families live in the kitchen, or in a room within another room downstairs, surrounded by their animals. The main food is grain that has been ground and roasted, so it can be eaten without boiling and baking. On sunny days people can escape to the roof and find a protected corner in the courtyard. When the sun sets, the whole household huddles around a tiny fire that's more smoke than heat, wearing three layers of homespun woolens. They scratch at lice, tell stories, and drink gallons of barley beer. It's a time-honored way to survive the smoke, the close quarters, and the cold. Winter, in short, is a test of creative survival.

A report by an Indian student of economics on the seven-month winter once concluded that most of the population was indigent, since hardly anyone has a paying job for seven months a year. The statistic was used to point out the people's backwardness and poverty. Helena disagreed. "In the West, when people don't work most of the time, we think they're rich. If they were Westerners the Ladakhis wouldn't be called unemployed. We'd say they were on vacation.

"The whole backbone of Western development is getting as much money in here as quickly as possible, without looking at the quality of life," Helena continued. "There's usually no vision of trying to plan for the long term in a way that's truly sustainable, in the same way that the original way of life is sustainable.

"You have Ladakhis who formerly were their own masters, farming, producing everything they needed for themselves, and then you develop. That means bringing women into Leh, where they sit from nine to five, all day long. Weaving. Is that improving their lives? Then the government can look on their charts and say, 'Now they're earning two rupees an hour. Before they weren't earning any money, poor people.' But the people didn't *need* money."

The country has been edging away from its traditional economy since 1947, when the first airstrip was built in Leh. Ladakh was threatened by the Pakistani army, so the Indian army needed a base near Leh. The airstrip was completed in ten days, with local labor and tools, and the first plane that landed, the story goes, was greeted with loads of hay, in case it was hungry.

"That's a story the Indians tell to make fun of the Ladakhis," said the head of the Leh farming cooperative. "The people didn't bring hay. They merely genuflected."

There are pressure cookers now, and kerosene heaters. People are switching to kerosene heaters because they are generally warmer, and even though kerosene comes on the black market from army stocks, it is easier to buy it than to gather dung. These are practical people—they don't stand on tradition when they're offered something they really need.

Nevertheless, it is hard to introduce something people don't think they need. Vegetables are a good example. Ngawang Tsering's grandfather, Sonam Lundup, who's still indefatigable in the fields, refuses to eat them. He lives on butter, meat, and roasted barley, and claims that vegetables make people weak. A Moravian missionary named Karl Marx tried to get the Ladakhis to eat potatoes a hundred years ago. Even though he started a baked-potato stall in the bazaar and gave them away for free, the people ignored him. They thought eating potatoes would automatically turn them into Christians.

A hundred years later, the head of the farming cooperative, R. N. Kalon, made the real change. When the army base expanded, he tried to persuade people to grow vegetables to supply the army. Although the people weren't interested, he went ahead on his own. When the vegetables were sold, he insisted upon payment in one-rupee notes. People weren't interested in vegetables, but they were fond of rupees. When they saw Kalon staggering home from the base under a sack of money, the vegetable market was born.

There are other highly touted innovations that don't do well. Fertilizer is a favorite panacea offered by the Indian army. When Prime Minister Nehru came to the army base to review the troops in 1962, he was appalled that there were people in his country who grew nothing but barley. He made it part of the army's policy there to teach people how to farm properly. The army had plenty of fertilizer to sell, but the people weren't buying. "It makes the vegetables grow large," Kalon reported, "but the fertilized vegetables do not taste as good. Also, fertilizer makes the soil hard and cracked. Now we only use fertilizer on the vegetables that we sell to the army, because the army will buy the giant vegetables. We save the good-tasting ones for ourselves."

Another Western invention, the flush toilet, is also slow to catch on, although tourists insist on them. The new hotels are all equipped, but the local people still prefer the old style. Ngawang Tsering's house has a traditional toilet: a hole in the second floor, separated from the rest of the house by a low wall and a gate, and open to the sunwashed sky. What falls to the ground floor is cleaned out regularly and composted. Nightsoil is the only kind of fertilizer Sonam Lundup will tolerate.

Ladakhis have always been parsimonious with their manure, careful with their fuel, and restrained in their marriages. The constant limiting factor is water. Ladakh is part of the central Asian dryland, a desert that starts at the shores of the Mediterranean and reaches over the continent all the way to North China. The monsoon rains only reach Ladakh by accident. Usually they're trapped by the gargantuan jumble of Himalayan peaks southeast of Ladakh.

The only available water comes from melting glaciers on the mountaintops. "It is always a problem," according to Tsering Norbu, who is the district forestry ranger for Leh. "Where the water flows, there is no [farming] land, because the water is in a gorge. Where there is land for farming, there is no water." Afforestation is his policy directive. He's been paying people to plant willow and poplar trees wherever the tiniest seep of water can be found.

Making the water work harder has been the goal of every Ladakhi farmer for thousands of years. Sonam Lundup did it about a decade ago, "in the year of the mouse," as he remembers. Nurla village is in a pocket-sized valley, and its irrigible land is all claimed. But three miles downriver the valley opens again, briefly. On the far side of the river is a large, flat area suitable for farming. Below it the river glides by, wet, unfettered, and out of reach. There is enough riverine deposit for three small barley fields and a tiny pasture.

"The problem," said Sonam Lundup, "has been that the river is down there and we are up here." In order to make this patch bloom, three families labored for two years to build a conduit from Nurla's own stream, three miles up the valley. The result is a long canal, just a bit wider than a man can straddle comfortably, lined with stone. Where the hard cliffs resisted their picks they built wooden scaffolds and lined the trough with rock and clay. If there was room, they planted poplars to hold the ditch in place. They carried basket after basket of composted dung to give the soil substance. After two or three years, the field was producing ten grains of barley for every one sown: in Ladakh, that's an acceptable return.

In the spring, the farmers draw straws for irrigation rights. There is so little water that they have to share the flow, shifting fields every few days. The arrangement is not foolproof, though.

Sonam Lundup is out walking the ditches each morning at four to rechannel the water back to his fields, because his neighbors have been there even earlier, secretly jockeying for the flow.

So far, bringing river water uphill to the fields is no more than an idea. The Indian government has been building a large dam at Stakna, upstream from Leh, since 1968. In 1978, disastrous floods washed out three-quarters of the completed work. When it is finished, acres now dry will be plantable. "There are one hundred thousand people in Ladakh now," said Tsering Norbu. "We could support two hundred thousand if we had the water."

But development proceeds. Ladakh has 113 villages. There are twenty-seven small-scale industries, with fifty-nine workers in them, and two cottage industries, with thirty-nine workers. There are 207 schools, with 6,369 students. There are twenty-two telephones, and fifty-five villages have water taps. More than 12,000 tourists visited Ladakh in 1980, and in Leh there were four crimes—two burglaries and two thefts.

"We used to make a big fire in the kitchen, and we would all sit around it and make handicrafts and shows, and people would tell stories," Thupstan Paldan, a monk working with the Leh Cultural Academy, remembers. "Now people have become very busy. Now they go to school, or they go to the handicraft center. It is a good change, but now there is no more passing down of stories. We don't want to change, but it's naturally changing. Before, we had a good time. People were free. There were no thieves; now there are many thieves. Before, the people were very religious; no more. Before there was no money; now everybody is running after money." His conclusion: "Money is very bad."

To Helena it seemed as if the Ladakhis were trading in their long-sustained self-sufficient society and their own happiness and peace of mind for the questionable benefits of modernity. Without realizing it, the Ladakhis were taking their paradise and subdividing it. "This doesn't have to be," she said. "To accept as inevitable the kind of development that cheapens a culture is more fatalistic than any thinking I've seen in the East.

"I can almost remember the exact day," she said. "It was in the summer of my first year in Ladakh. I was lying in a grassy field outside of Leh, and suddenly I sat straight up. I almost shouted. I realized that it *doesn't* have to be! Development isn't like nature. It's not inevitable, like the seasons. Development is just beginning here. Suddenly I realized that if there's anywhere on earth that can be developed in a way that's *sustainable,* in tune with the earth, it's right here in Ladakh!"

Her first thought was to save the country by limiting tourism. She wrote letters to the national government and to the state government of Jammu and Kashmir, in which she pointed out what was at stake. "Traditional life in Ladakh is strikingly similar to Gandhi's utopia," she wrote, "but he believed that this ideal had only existed in the agrarian villages of ancient India. Gandhi saw a republic of small villages, each of them self-sufficient, where each person would do his bread labor and also work for the community as a whole. Laws and restraints would be minimal, crime wouldn't exist, and neither would discrimination by wealth, sex, or religion. There would be a true democracy, since communities would be small enough for each person to have a say. Everyone would have an equally valuable role to play in society, and no one would benefit at the expense of another."

The response to her letters was negligible. Tourism could not be restructured: the moneyed interests were already entrenched. In a great intuitive leap, Helena decided that the best way to maintain the Ladakhi culture would be by offering them a kind of development that would enhance their lives without costing them their self-sufficiency, and she decided to do it herself. The environmental constraints were in her favor; the weather closes the country for most of the year, and without labor and transportation year-round, there's no incentive for large industries in the country. Natural resources are limited. The settlements are widespread, so centralization and mass communication are impossible. “The traditional structure here fits beautifully with small-is-beautiful ideas,” said Helena.

If there's anything Helena excels in, it's talking to people in their own language. In London, she talked to the Intermediate Technology Group, a foundation started by E. F. Schumacher, author of *Small is Beautiful.* It presented her with a grant and an engineer, and they set about building Trombe walls. A Trombe wall is a simple solar collector, designed by a French engineer and most useful in cold places where there is sunshine to spare. It is a double brick wall whose interstice is filled with an insulator, such as straw. Four vents are built into the wall, two at ceiling level and two on the floor. The outside face of the wall is painted black, and about four inches from it is a window of double-paned glass. Sunshine goes through the glass and heats the black wall thoroughly, raising the temperature within the four-inch space enough to allow convection. Standing behind the Trombe wall, one can feel the hot air pouring into the room through the ceiling vent, and the cold air flowing into the warmed space behind the window through the floor vents. The heat the wall absorbs keeps the room warm for up to three days.

It's a simple idea, easily grasped by people in this nontechnical culture. People have explained the idea to one another using the same word for convection that they use to describe the circumambulation of a religious shrine. Because the sun only shines on the black wall, the carpets won't fade. Helena has calculated that a family can equip a house with a Trombe wall for roughly what it would receive from selling a yak. Ladakhis don't think much about pay-back periods, but the people of Leh will spend the same amount on coal or kerosene heating in two or three years.

Helena was helped by two important local people. Sonam Norbu, the fabled engineer of the road and the airstrip, was by then influential in the Jammu and Kashmir government. He supported Helena enthusiastically. The first Trombe wall was installed on a house he owned in Leh. (It was to be the last engineering project he would oversee before he died.)

In Leh, Helena was helped by Tashi Robgyas, Ladakh's most respected Buddhist scholar, who is the local information officer for the Jammu and Kashmir government. He lives, when in town, in a small apartment overlooking Leh's bazaar. From his rooftop the Indus can be seen, a tinsel streak in the valley below. He wrote a song about Helena and her message: "Helena came from the West. In the West there are many industries, but they don't have our happy peace of mind. What's more important than that? Working with animals makes friendship. Working with machines is working with dead things, and it makes you dead yourself."

He has given Helena's alternative technology message a particularly Buddhist slant. "We will be going ahead of the twentieth century through Buddhism," he said. "Only now is the West realizing the limitations beyond which it cannot progress. We knew this two thousand years ago. Reason is the basis of our cultural wisdom, and the basis for science as well. And thus there is no contradiction between the two. If there is the good will of Buddhism, then all things scientific and technical will be useful.

"In my childhood, I never looked at the rest of the world, and when I look back, it was very beautiful. But you cannot live without change. You cannot live isolated. If you study the history of nations, you find that people become so fascinated by change that they don't care anymore about their old culture. In Ladakh we know how to keep this in view."

Two model Trombe walls went up in the summer of 1979. "They proved to be extremely successful," Helena reported. "Both rooms were used throughout the winter without any supplementary heating." The next summer, with money from the British High Commission—a small grant amounting to less than

$1,500—she underwrote the construction of three Trombe walls in Sabu, a village about three miles from Leh. By now she had to choose the places carefully, because she already had more requests than she could fill.

The only purpose of the Trombe wall is for heating; cooking is still done over dung fires or on kerosene burners. Yet the wall's advantages are distinct. "It's amazing; there doesn't seem to be anything wrong with it," said John Page. He is a tall Englishman who went to Ladakh for a visit in 1979 and fell for the country, for Helena, and for her ideas. "A Ladakhi family can now go for a whole winter without buying fuel," he said. "Some people used to spend 1,500 rupees a winter on kerosene. It's absurd to start running this country on kerosene when the sun shines 320 days a year."

"Heating is the only serious problem the Ladakhis face," Helena said. "People spend most of the winter in a dark, smoky room, huddled around a small fire. Almost all their diseases are respiratory and eye and rheumatism, and these can be traced to smoke and insufficient heat. In the areas that have been developed, and particularly in Leh, the kerosene and coke are a mixed blessing. Because of the difficulty and expense of getting supplies up to Leh, people in these areas have at times found themselves worse off than the traditional villagers, and all the signs are that things will not improve."

The road into Leh takes a sharp left turn, and then a sharp right, just before entering the main bazaar. Overlooking the left turn, with a clear view all the way down the slope, is a house belonging to a man who serves tea in the district commissioner's office. On the first floor are shops, and on the second floor was a gaping hole which was fast becoming a demonstration solar collector. "In 1981," said Page, "we got some money for solar projects, and we were thinking of putting a wall in a house in one of the villages along the road. But then it seemed as if we were working very hard and not getting anywhere, so we thought we'd put one where everyone could see it. And that meant Leh.

"We went to this man and said we'd provide three thousand rupees, and no more, if we could fix his house up with a wall. He said, go ahead, and there will be no problem, and there hasn't been. It's been like this through all our work here. You can't get more obvious than this. Every day people stop and ask about it. They want to know why we have to take the old wall down, why we're painting the new one black and what the straw is for. They're really interested. I can hear them down in the market below explaining it to each other."

Page has been a diligent overseer, in the market every morning to check the progress of the wall. Progress is fitful. The best-trained Ladakahi carpentry crew wasn't available, so he trained a new one. When they tore the old wall out the dust was thick, even for Leh. The builders' first mistake was putting the Trombe wall itself at the edge of the construction, with no room for the window. A day was lost. The wall itself went up easily, except for the innovative picture window the builders thought to put in its center, and the mud they tried to substitute for straw as insulation. Two more days lost. Page and Helena wanted the final window to be decorated as in so many Ladakhi houses, but the people of this family are Shia Moslems, and their religion forbids decoration. Even undecorated, though, the solar collector is hard to miss: the windows are gleaming and backed by solid black. It's the first thing anybody sees on the way into Leh's bazaar.

By the end of the summer of 1982, Helena had helped to put up twenty Trombe walls. Six had gone up without her help or money. The idea is spreading, in a small, beautiful way: the Indian Development Commission has recognized the value of her work and has given over the land for a small-is-beautiful education center in Leh. Besides keeping a library, the center is also staging a comedy written by Thupstan Paldan, the monk. It is a modern morality tale: a Ladakhi family sells everything, down to its copper kettle, to pay to send its eldest son to school in Kashmir. But the result of the boy's education is unanticipated. The boy comes home in blue jeans with a radio in his ear, and he wants white bread and flush toilets. His parents' life won't satisfy him. He is especially insolent to his grandfather and insists, when the grandfather falls ill, on passing over the familiar *amche.* Instead he brings in a doctor who trained in America for seven years. But the doctor treats the old man with herbs! The doctor explains that in America, people actually pay to take a walk. There everyone had offered him money for the herbal cures he had practiced in Ladakh. "There all the people would tell me I'm so lucky to be a Ladakhi," he said.

But not all Ladakhis are as disillusioned with what the West has to offer as is Helena. "Normally the people who want the villages not to change are the Western intellectuals," said the manager of the Indian airlines office. "But not to change means to be devoid of education, devoid of modern facilities. Some Westerners are very nostalgic about the past. They think the past is good, that modern is bad. These ideas must be balanced."

In the traditional Ladakhi way, Tashi Robgyas puts things in philosophical perspective. "Buddhists accept change as natural law," he says. "Nothing remains static. Every phenomenon is subject to change. Becoming a Buddha is the greatest change. Without change, we cannot become a Buddha. So people here invite change, and every change has been positive."

CHAPTER SEVEN

The Medicine Rocks

A HIGH, softly rounded ball of a mountain that glints with green serpentine gravel, Peak Eight (5,193 feet) is the center of the universe for the Yurok, Karuk, and Tolowa people. The Klamath River is the southern boundary of that universe. Where it enters the Siskiyou Mountains of northwestern California it is a dry-land river, narrow and banked with willow. By the time the river reaches the old Yurok village site at Weitchpec, though, the hills have steepened into mountains and the Klamath is wide and eager, feeding on melted snow. At Weitchpec it merges with the Trinity River, takes a right turn, and heads northwest instead of southwest. The Klamath's path, a westerly pointing arm bent at the elbow, used to be all the orientation the Karuk Indians needed. Their riverine compass had six points: upriver, downriver, uphill, downhill, this side of the river, and across the river. Even the name "Karuk" means "upriver" in Yurok; "Yurok" means "downriver."

The Klamath, it seems, existed before the mountains it flows through. Perhaps for this reason it has cut a female landscape. Instead of sharp peaks piling toward the sky, there is a more subtle silhouette of almost catenary curves yielding to deeply scored valleys. In these tangled mountains the rivers have always offered the only natural route from here to there, as well as being the most habitable land. Medicine men and women prayed in the high country, but the other Indians used to make their homes along the river. Because they were herded for so long into the Hupa Valley Indian Reservation along the Trinity and Klamath rivers, many Yurok and Karuk Indians still do.

The hills that can be seen from the river are bunked among rounded ridges, the uplifted beaches of a prehistoric ocean. Geologists say that these mountains have at three different times been submerged beneath the sea, only to be squeezed skyward again. The Indians, on the other hand, say the hills were submerged only once, when a deluge flooded all the land around the Klamath except for the center of the universe, the peaks hidden back in the Siskiyou mountains within the elbow of the Klamath—above the trees, safe from the flood-mad river.

In the high country, a few unusual but not very imposing landforms punctuate a medium-sized ridge. These are the legendary medicine rocks of the Yurok and Karuk Indians. Chimney Rock (5,727 feet) is a small protuberance of weatherworn red rock. Nearby is the bare and rusty hilltop known as Turtle Rock. Doctor Rock (4,924 feet) is not far north of them, a small brushy dome from which a monument-sized boulder rises like a podium. In the protected crack of this boulder is a soot-blackened grotto littered with beer cans—a medicine cave. Only in the high country can medicine men and women pray for the rooted steadiness that countervails when the universe is knocked out of balance by human foolishness. Visions are clearest at the knobby tops of the modest mountains that swelled up near a peak called Doctor Rock, Ha-ag-ah-klau. Rock upon rock. This is the place where a few select Yurok women can go questing for visions, after which they return to the villages to train with older women as doctors. Overshadowed by Doctor Rock, Ah Kah, Bad Place, is where men stand to call down bad luck upon their enemies. As often as not, the incantation backfires and the curser finds himself cursed. At Chimney Rock, men pray for wisdom and strength, and the medicine men pray for a power they can shoot down to the people on the river like a shaft of light. The tribes used to pray by dancing the Jump

Dance and the White Deerskin Dance of World Renewal—standing in a long line, they stamped their feet on the ground to balance the world. Guided by the medicine men, they prayed for law. When the law was broken, the universe blistered with sickness and storm, insanity and murder. To this day Yurok people believe the world is in turmoil because of individual wrongdoing. A lawbreaker is seized by a bad luck that shakes him into humility, for when the law is broken, the balance needs to be found again. This Indian religion is no once-a-week genuflection; it is a voice of the universe, with the power to make itself heard.

"Lots of people laugh at the Indian beliefs," Sam Jones has said. "I've seen where it works." Sam is a full-blooded Yurok in his seventies who still lives in the dark, high-ceilinged house his grandfather built on the Klamath at Martin's Ferry, near Weitchpec. He tells a story about a young fellow trying to set himself up as a medicine man. The young man headed for the sacred high country to strike up an acquaintance with the Great Spirit, but he hadn't prayed and abstained and fasted first, hadn't obeyed the law. He ran across a bear and was chased off course. The young apprentice medicine man was lost for two or three days, and finally emerged gaunt and betwigged sixty miles from his destination. Sam chuckles over the story. "Our Indian belief," he says, "is that he's lucky he got out of it alive." When the old-time Indians trained, he says, they could walk from Weitchpec to Doctor Rock easily, partly because the forests were burned out each year. "When you train," says Sam, "you can do lots of things you feel like you couldn't do. You feel like you're super." But, he adds, lots of young people aren't up to the fasting and sexual abstention that readies them for a vision quest in the high country.

Someone who is called to a vision quest actually starts questing at that moment; the climb and sojourn in the mountains are but the culmination of a long struggle. Along the trail the quester finds power in everything, from stones and feathers to pieces of gnawed-over skeleton half buried in the duff. Charlie Thom, a Karuk medicine man and one of the few knowledgeable Indians of the Klamath region who will talk about spiritual affairs, teaches that all living things—rocks, shellfish, trees, mountains—are brothers and sisters: the whole teeming universe is interconnected. Yurok tradition has it that the *wogey,* the "before-time people" who lived on earth before the human beings, retreated to the high country when the people came, hiding from them by turning themselves into rocks, streams, and animals. Some of them ascended through a hole in the sky, and there is a place near the medicine rocks where their last footprints can still be seen. The rest turned themselves into trees.

The trees in these damp, warm mountains grow in bewildering variety, making perhaps the most genetically marbled forest on earth, rivaled only by places in the Himalaya, half a globe away. Oak, alder, and maple live here, and twenty different kinds of conifer. Unusual plants have colonized the acidic serpentine soils, like the cobra lily, which sucks from insects what the soil denies it. Along the Indian trails from the villages to the high country, for those who can see them, there are prayer seats where a quester can pause, prepare, and take account of a living moment in a 16-million-year-old forest.

* * * * *

The forest lost a powerful protector in 1984 with the death of a knowledgeable and highly respected elder, Lowana Brantner, whom many knew as Princess Lowana. The title had come to her when, as a young woman, she had been chosen for the court of the Queen of the Redwood Empire by the famous Indian athlete, Jim Thorpe. Lowana liked to think it was her patrician Yurok ancestry that made the name stick. A petite, fragile, and attractive Yurok woman in her late seventies, she had been raised by her Yurok grandmother to be a living encyclopedia of Yurok lore. She owned a large collection of woodpecker scalps and the feathered, antique dance regalia worn in traditional Yurok religious dances, and she knew how to keep them in repair. (This skill may have disappeared altogether with her death.) She could remember and liked to sing the lucky songs her grandfather had learned on one pilgrimage to Chimney Rock, although she always apologized for her own high, thin tone when she sang. Her grandfather's voice, she would say, had echoed just like a canyon. Lowana was not one of the famous Yurok woman doctors who had trained on Doctor Rock, but her grandmothers had been, and Lowana claimed to have walked until there were blisters on her feet accompanying them there. Although Lowana never trained as a doctor, she knew how to make medicine. Lowana's house on the Klamath River beside Mettah Creek lay so deeply in the gorge that she could not see the medicine rocks, but when she prayed she preferred to "aim" in that direction; she oriented herself by two tall trees on the top of the ridge across the river.

In recent years, Lowana had lost her health to a pernicious bone cancer. Her skin had yellowed, and her vivacious energy had begun to ebb. She was traveling to visit the doctor when the accident took place. Her close friends, Sam and Audrey Jones, were driving her to town on the road down the twisting Trinity River canyon when a double-trailer chip truck, straddling both lanes as it rounded a bend, crushed the Joneses' station wagon and its three occupants. Audrey Jones can drive again, although it isn't easy for her, but Sam, who was in the back seat, was incapacitated by the hip injuries he sustained. Sam is a solemn, bulky, thick-necked man who, before the accident, looked much younger than his seventy-some years. Like Lowana, he is a hereditary tribal leader who takes his responsibilities seriously.

The three elders had been awaiting a decision from the federal appeals court on the Gasquet-Orleans road, or "GO road," as it is known. For over a dozen years Sam and other Yurok and Karuk leaders had been trying to persuade the U.S. Forest Service not to build this logging road right through the high country, through the one section of the mountains that the Indian people revered above all others. Although it was designed to carry all kinds of traffic, the GO road's main mission, according to officials in the coastal counties, was as a delivery route to bring mountain timber to mills on the coast. In this impoverished and isolated region the Forest Service felt a strong obligation to provide timber to the mills that are the mainstay of the regional economy.

It was because of the timber that Sam and Lowana were in the minority in not wanting the road to be built. In a 1981 Del Norte County referendum, voters from such places as Gasquet, Requa, and Crescent City voted by a four-to-one margin in favor of the road. Among these voters were Yurok, Karuk, and Tolowa Indians who preferred paychecks to prayers. Most of these people had at one time been taught that the sacred high country was the spiritual heart of the Indian world, but many of them had run out of unemployment benefits and were getting clear messages from their former employers that the slump had come because all the timber was locked up in the mountains, with no road to haul it.

Before the accident, Sam and Lowana used to sit at the table in the dim dining room at Sam's house, calling up old beliefs and confirming them in the language of the Yurok. Sam might recall the word for "fish," and they'd discuss for a moment, in English, whether it meant "fish swimming" or "fish to eat." Of all the words they remembered, one of the hardest to translate was the word that indicated the spirit sought by questers in the mountains. The word for "spirit" means, all at once, "sky," "world," "earth," and "universe." It means "that which exists" and "you and me." In a sense, then, it refers to *reality.*

Lowana and Sam were determined to maintain a spiritual

home, a sense of that reality, for their people—whether the majority of Yuroks knew they needed it or not. Sky, earth, universe—Sam and Lowana's reality is clear to anyone who stands on top of Doctor Rock on a sparkling, sunny day. To the west is the ocean and the fog-shrouded coast; to the east hangs Mount Shasta's snow-capped cone, rising alone from the haze-obscured valley. The Karuk medicine tradition teaches that you don't show respect for a mountain by sitting on top of it; you do it honor by going where it can be seen. From the top of Doctor Rock you can see Shasta, as well as the Siskiyous, the Klamaths, the Trinity Alps. The viewshed of Doctor Rock includes an entire universe.

"If you're praying up there," Sam Jones once explained, "you look west when the sun goes down. If you see the blue light, then your prayers are answered. But if you're praying on Doctor Rock, and you open your eyes and look, and it's all logged off," he continued, "then you don't get nothing."

* * * * *

The decision to roll the GO road through the sacred high country, and to sell off the timber the road would give access to, lay with the Six Rivers National Forest, whose headquarters is in the coastal town of Eureka. As far as the five forest supervisors who have held the position since the GO road controversy warmed up are concerned, the Indians upriver in the mountains were expecting miracles. The national forests aren't in business to set up private shrines, and as a "land of many uses," as all its road signs proclaim, Six Rivers had a fistful of special interests to placate.

Besides the Indians' protests, Six Rivers National Forest had been criticized by conservationists for its logging and roading plans. Intense winter storms, unstable rock, and historically disastrous logging practices have left the watersheds in these mountains with some of the highest erosion rates in the world. Wilderness lovers complained that Six Rivers persistently slated irreplaceable watersheds full of rare plants and animals for timber sales. Fishermen were upset by the destruction of salmon spawning streams by the sediment that washes down from clearcuts to clog the gravel beds where salmon lay eggs, and by the salmon fry's potentially lethal exposure to the increased stream temperatures that come when logging takes the shade along with the trees. On the other hand, the mill owners and county officials at Del Norte, for whom Six Rivers is primarily a timber bank, were impatient with Six Rivers whenever it bowed to pressure from the environmentalists. If that weren't enough, Six Rivers had been chastised to the courts by failing to fulfill the complicated procedures set by law that are supposed to help it pick its way through all these conflicting demands. Lawsuits have become an unwelcome part of the daily routine at Six Rivers.

Legitimate users were not the only people making demands on the Six Rivers National Forest. Several times in the last few years, callers identifying themselves as radical environmentalists had telephoned bomb threats to the office. Defense measures, such as locked doors, identification badges, and strict security became another unwelcome fact of life at the beleaguered office. Since the market for the mills' timber had nearly dried up, some people had begun to harvest another crop—marijuana—in the national forest. The marijuana growers were a serious threat to the Six Rivers staff; foresters had had to dodge bullets, hand grenades, and booby traps. (Ordinary backpackers had gone into the forest and never returned.) Some growers came from outside the area, but others were local people, some calling themselves environmentalists, who joined with the more legitimate interests to harass the Forest Service.

The herbicide issue is a good example of Six Rivers being at odds with several groups over one issue. Herbicides like the commonly used 2,4-D phenoxy, sprayed from airplanes over large swathes of cut-over land, will shrivel the broadleaf plants they land on, and marijuana is particularly susceptible. However, until a recent court order stopped the practice, the Forest Service regularly sent planes over its newly planted clearcuts. It's a common technique, used most often on privately held timber land, that is supposed to encourage the newly planted fir seedlings to grow faster by poisoning the broadleaf weeds and shrubs that normally would overgrow them and block their sunlight. But remote clearcuts are ideal marijuana fields, and growers were upset. They sided with fishermen, who saw that phenoxy herbicides washing into the streams were hurting the fish; with environmentalists, who pointed out that herbaceous trees and brush were nature's Band-Aid to stop erosion on newly cleared land; with Indians, who lost their acorn crop, herbs, and grasses to the spray; and with hunters, who worried about the health of the animals they shot. Hunting in this money-short region is how people put meat on their tables. "The deer I shoot up there," says Sam Jones, "the liver is so blistered up you can't even eat it."

Six Rivers personnel were unable to distinguish among these factions and saw them all as potential harassers, possibly dangerous. Criticism and bad press were seen to have pushed an ordinarily relaxed, open Forest Service headquarters into a defensive position behind closed doors. The baseline work of managing the forest—monitoring its health, protecting it from fire and disease, serving the people who used and lived in it, selling its timber—was as much as possible hidden from public view. While it followed the letter of the law that required it to accept public comment on the decisions it made, Six Rivers made its own judgements behind closed doors.

It was no secret to Six Rivers that the GO road, originally cut as a fire trail by a Civilian Conservation Corps crew in the 1930s, had for the crew's convenience been laid to follow the

Indian trails that led straight across the mountains to the heart of the high country. In the 1960s, as well, Forest Service engineers made plans to upgrade and hard-top the old fire trail knowing full well that some Indians didn't appreciate the idea. But the planners had other priorities in mind.

Since the Second World War, the north coastal counties' fortunes have risen and fallen with timber. The GO road was far more than a shortcut from Gasquet to Orleans; it was Del Norte's highway to the forest that allowed Del Norte mills to bid on timber in a wider radius, log it, haul it in and mill it, and haul it out. The GO road would provide a short route that would shrink haulage costs for Del Norte mills, and it would open up a backcountry vault of 3.25 billion board feet of timber.

The GO road was but one of the roads that were planned for the area. Hundreds of miles of logging roads were expected to twine around the high country, and much of the old forest was earmarked for cutting. By making the high country and its surroundings available to timber sales, the Forest Service was responding to two kinds of pressures. The first was an unprecedented national demand for housing. When the Forest Service made its first plans to upgrade the fire trail into the GO road, the California northwest was in the midst of a timber boom the likes of which hadn't been seen before, and haven't been seen since. The GO road was integral to a timber transportation plan that in the 1960s seemed inevitable. In the 1950s and 1960s, the population doubled in Del Norte County, and nearly doubled in Humboldt. The mills were turning out plywood, chips, and boards. North coast Douglas fir shot through the mills and was shipped to San Francisco, where it was turned into suburban houses and painted pink.

A plan is just an idea on paper, though, and it can be changed. Regarding the GO road, Six Rivers had its honor at stake. The GO road had been promised to Del Norte county in 1967 when the Forest Service tried to balance a compromise between environmentalists on the one hand and economic interests on the other, in a deal that traded the fir in the high country for the redwood trees on the coast. When a new Redwood National Park was under consideration in Humboldt and Del Norte counties in 1967, Ronald Reagan, then governor of California, opposed the plan. "A tree's a tree—how many more do you need to look at?" he had quipped. But he did offer to back down if jobs could be protected. In response to Governor Reagan's request, the Johnson Administration directed the Forest Service Chief to increase the annual allowable cut from the Six Rivers National Forest; the chief told Congress that this could be done, and that the GO road, once completed, could be used to haul the timber out. The Del Norte County Board of Supervisors read the chief's statement as a promise, and still regards the road as a debt Six Rivers has left unpaid.

Without realizing it, redwood conservationists had handed over the spiritual center of the Yurok universe for a Redwood National Park with signposts indicating precisely where, why, and how its visitors should feel awed.

At that time, the Six Rivers management felt justified in the way it had passed over Indian belief. Indian people were just as dependent on the timber industry as were the rest of the people in the counties. Sam Jones had been a timber faller when the crews sawed the trees down by hand. Lowana Brantner claimed to have been the first female logger in the country. Some of the worst timber practices around could be seen on the reservation, and disputes over the proceeds from reservation timber sales had kept the Yurok feuding for years with the Hupa. Nor was there consensus even among the Yurok as to the exact nature of its mountain-mediated spiritual rapport with the Great Creator. Some thought Lowana's view was too simplistic. "There's some people who don't like me sticking my nose in this business," she had said, referring to her role in the GO road suit. "But when you're a princess in the tribe, you've got to do these things."

Even Charlie Thom had been slow to take a stand against the road—he had been on the survey crew when the GO road was first laid out. There is a rumor that the survey boss had asked Thom whether it wouldn't bother the Indians to have a road cut through the sacred high country, and that Thom had said it would make no difference. Thom was a young man then, an experienced logger who could run and repair any machine that would fit on a mountain when he was sober. Like many of his people, he was a strong, massive man whose huge chest dwarfed his muscular arms and legs. As a man against another man in single combat he could defend himself, but as an Indian in a white world he generally lost. If Charlie Thom told the survey boss that it didn't matter what the Indians thought, he was speaking from experience.

* * * * *

What the Forest Service—as well as the Del Norte County Supervisors and some mill operators—could not understand is how those knobby peaks ruled the hearts of Sam, Lowana, and others who had taken upon themselves the guidance of their people. Lowana had been raised in both the Christian and Indian traditions and had managed to blend them in a way that, for her, presented no contradictions. She would paraphrase the Bible: "I raise my eyes to the mountains from whence comes my strength." Then she would explain, "God gave us Doctor Rock, that overlooks the ocean and all the country east, west, north, and south, so that we can go and pray in these places. The God of the Indians and the whites is the same. We have to let him know that we need him."

Yurok and Karuk people have never had the kind of traditional belief in God that would give them reason to say, "He walks with me and He talks with me" in the daily course of their lives. Only medicine men and women praying in the high country had that privilege. Nor did their daily lives include obeisances to minor dieties in the court of the Great Creator, even though the very grasses and stones were soaked with religious significance.

What the Yurok and Karuk people do have is a religious system that gives them a sense of spiritual companionship that expresses itself everywhere. As Charlie Thom says, it's stones and feathers and streams that make up the Indian Bible. The Yurok and Karuk medicine people, perhaps fifteen people in a community that numbers several thousand, are the ones that interpret that Bible. They are the only people equipped to touch the Great Spirit and beam the power from the medicine rocks to the people waiting below. If they lost the places where spiritual communications took place, Sam and Lowana's people would be losing their bond as a community. They put momentous stake in saving their sacred mountain lands because it was their only chance to avoid exile from their god and from one another. They knew if the light went out and the spirit stopped talking, they really would be alone.

"We need those mountains where we pray," Lowana had said. "That's where God's spirit remains to speak to you and to help you. Just ask Him."

That the Indian religion has survived at all might be seen as some kind of miracle. According to Sam Jones, the first Indians killed when the whites came to northern California in the gold rush of the 1850s were the medicine people. The Indians called the white men "dog eaters" when they first found the whites unable to catch anything but the semitame Indians' dogs for meat. The derision didn't last. In the 1860s and 1870s, an Indian found alone in the mountains might be used for target practice. The killing of a white by an Indian, on the other hand, would trigger a massive retaliation—perhaps the massacre of an entire Indian village. In 1860, 183 women and children of the Wiyot tribe were killed on an island off Eureka as they slept, in retribution for Indian raids on the cattle that were grazing off seed-bearing grasses that were the Indians' traditional winter harvest. By 1870 many of the Indians were either dead or restricted to reservations. In the 1970s these events remained as a living memory among Yurok and Karuk elders.

Thanks to white colonization, the traditional way of life along the river became difficult. Placer miners in search of gold had rifled at the riverside slopes with huge hydraulic hoses to pan the gold from the dirt, thoroughly burying the gravel-bedded spawning streams in silt. Lumbermen cleared the forests down to the very edge of the rivers and cut roads that the drenching winter rains regraded as gullies. Lumbermen shoved brush and branches into the creeks to make bridges for their tractors. These were known as Humboldt crossings, and the Forest Service to this day has crews in the woods trying to clear them out. As a result of these disturbances, stream channels filled and lifted by tens of feet in some places. The once prolific salmon and steelhead have been all but exterminated in the drainages of the Klamath and its tributaries. Documents from the turn-of-the-century cannery at the mouth of the Klamath talk of salmon so plentiful they were pitchforked ashore. In 1985, only twenty-two thousand of this run that once numbered half a million made it upstream to spawn. Today there is serious talk of stripping the Indians of their right to fish in the Klamath.

The Yurok believe that the world is in turmoil because of things people have done wrong. Charlie Thom says that what we see now—"floods and earthquakes, girls kissing girls, and animals acting strange"—is but a foretaste of the future. The white pioneers of the last century explained the disorder they saw in another way: "There is no law north of the Mad River. There is no God north of the Klamath."

Sam Jones and Lowana Brantner grew up after the Indian Wars, as they were called by the whites, had stopped. They had a different kind of experience. "It was the next thing they tried when they found they couldn't kill us all, to try to make us forget we were Indian," said Sam in an uncharacteristically bitter remark. In their childhoods, it was the practice of the Bureau of Indian Affairs to send the Indian children to far-off schools where they might learn how to act like white people. Lowana herself went to school in southern California. Other children were stashed in hollow trees while their parents and grandparents denied their existence to the authorities. In local Indian schools, children were severely punished for speaking their own language. The crippled arm of one of the more fluent speakers of the Tolowa language is the legacy of a zealous teacher who punished her for speaking Tolowa in school. Her parents, terrified of further punishment, never tended it.

Linguistic evidence indicates that the Yurok, Karuk, and Tolowa people arrived in the Klamath and Smith River Mountains at different times and from widely diverging locales. The Yurok speak an Algonquian language related to the languages spoken by Indians in Nova Scotia and New England. The Tolowa language is in the Athabascan, or Dene language family that has echoes to the north in the subarctic and to the south in the American desert. The Karuks speak a language in the Hokan family that extends farther south into Mexico. None of the tribes has ever had a written language; in the old days children learned by watching and listening. As an adult even Lowana, who was absent from her boarding school for months on end, found the Yurok language and all it represented a little fuzzy. Today Sam and Audrey Jones are raising Sam's young teenage nephews. Sam rarely speaks directly to the boys, and they rarely ask him questions. Instead he sits, as he used to with Lowana, in the dark dining room discussing the day's happenings and judging them by the standards of Yurok law, certain that the boys could be found overhead, peering from the stairwell, listening. Out of necessity, the conversations are conducted in English. His was the last generation to hear Yurok spoken at home.

The white community was for the most part blind to these struggles. "Some of our own Indian people, they say that the white man is teaching this and teaching that, and so they don't want to do the old Indian things," Sam often complains. "They think, What's the use of following the Indian way? Right up to the present day there's people trying to break our culture." Until just a few years ago, most white people in the region had mentally deposited the Indian culture in the past, with the baskets, shells, and deerskin dresses in the Eureka museum. When Sam and others started filing objections against the GO road with the Forest Service, that agency had some serious discussions over whether it was the Sierra Club, which in 1968 had begun to organize support for establishing a Siskiyou Wilderness, that had put the Indians up to it.

* * * * *

Sam made no formal protests to the Forest Service until the GO road had already rolled tens of miles into the high country. It had been built a section at a time and paid for in piecemeal allotments granted by Congress, which was never able to muster enough money to fund the road in its entirety. The first public hearing for the road was staged by the Forest Service in 1973. Outside in the parking lot were out-of-work loggers and men wielding knives to remind everyone that the Forest Service had promised that road. Inside were about 150 people taking their first opportunity since the road was first conceived, almost forty years before, to vent their opinions. Up in the mountains were forty-three miles of nicely engineered, winding highway built in sections that often were named for timber sales that they accessed. Only two sections, the Dillon-Flint, 6.8 miles, and the 6.2-mile Chimney Rock, the linchpin of the road, remained to be built. As it stood, the asphalt ended not a mile from Doctor Rock. Beer cans had already begun to pile up in the tiny grotto.

"There are no places which have equivalent functions in white cultures, except perhaps the pilgrimage destinations in Palestine, Mecca, and Jerusalem. Or maybe the great cathedrals of Europe," Sam Jones and other Indians wrote in a letter to Six Rivers. The universe was their cathedral: it wasn't just certain points on the map that needed protection, but the entire peaked and valleyed landscape. The medicine rocks would stay sacred only as long as the viewshed there, all the trees, streams, plants, and animals, stayed the same as they had always been. As Charlie Thom put it, "The Great Creator put everything on this earth right where he wanted it because he had a need for it there. It's none of our business to go in and change things around." The point was duly noted by the Forest Service, but the protection of 13.5 billion board feet of timber in order to please a few elderly Indians up in the mountains was not within departmental protocol. The following Thanksgiving, two hikers in the high country discovered crews clearing the right-of-way for the Dillon-Flint section of trees. In a determination to keep to its original timetable, Six Rivers had proceeded with bidding and contracting in secret. "Me and the Forest Service got in a growl with each other after that," Sam remembers.

* * * * *

There are different kinds of medicine for the Yurok and Karuk, and they are made by different kinds of medicine people. Lowana's grandmothers were famous women doctors who not only treated sick people but also conducted ceremonies that kept small children from becoming sick. This ceremony is called the Brush Dance. The way Sam describes it, the Brush Dance makes medicine that sets a baby off in the right direction. People line up and dance by stamping their feet, Sam says, to stamp out the bad spirits so the good ones can come in. All the young Yurok men, Sam included, had Brush Dances held for them before they went to fight in the Second World War. Anthropologist Arnold Pilling reports that one Yurok man taught the vigorous steps of the Brush Dance to his fellow soldiers, who used them to warm up before they fought the Battle of the Bulge. Sam says that everyone who had the Brush Dance danced in his honor came back from the war. Today Brush Dances are performed by a Wintu Indian doctor, Florence Jones, who lives far from the Klamath near Mount Shasta. Sam himself always turns to her for medicine and advice, for within his own Yurok culture there are no more doctors.

Men who make medicine perform different functions. The elderly Yurok "chief" Dewey George, for example, used to go to the high country to pray for the health of his community. He infuriated a few people when he said he favored the GO road. With his advanced age and failing health, he figured that the only way he would ever see the high country again would be by riding up there in his car. Other medicine people cast spells, pray for the dead, and conduct ceremonies. For the most part, these people like to be anonymous. Sam explains that it spoils the medicine if people watch you praying, or even know you're doing it. This attitude caused some confusion in the Forest Service, which in 1974, in response to pressures from Sam and his friends, began to look into the issue of Indian religion. A young Forest Service archaeologist interviewed dozens of Indians, asking them to comment on the cultural significance of the outcrops, ridges, and rocks that make up the medicine rocks. Their answers were vague. People would say they remembered their grandparents using it in the old days. What the archaeologist never discovered was that while he shuttled up and down the river asking questions, there was a medicine man up in the high country praying for a boy who had recently died. When the archaeologist talked to the boy's family, they never mentioned it.

Charlie Thom, who has no such compunction against talking to the Forest Service, to journalists, or to anyone else who will listen, is more interested in what he calls "touch the earth" medicine, and says that it's Indian prayer that's behind laws that require environmental impact statements and sane forestry practices. "We have the Great Spirit behind us," he says. "That's because everything we do, we ask. We don't take unless we ask."

Charlie Thom doesn't speak in paragraphs. His statements tend to flow from thought to related thought, the way Lowana's did. He is a few years younger than Sam Jones, and has a gaze that fixes his listeners as if they were mosquitoes and he a hungry bullfrog. He had been raised on the river by his grandparents, who were Karuk leaders. His medicine-man grandfather trained Charlie for the job, and Charlie remembers being hauled up to the medicine rocks roped to the back of a mule when he was just four years old. It's almost a code among the Yurok and Karuk to say that someone grew up on the river; it means that they were raised in the traditional way and learned how to weave nets and fish for salmon, how to hollow out redwood logs without splitting them, how to weave baskets, which willows to cut and at what time of the year, where the best acorns could be gathered, how to make dye out of maidenhair fern. A child raised on the river knew the real names of places, and which places were powerful. Charlie Thom never left the river until he was drafted to fight in the Second World War. As a medicine man trained to keep the universe in balance, Charlie was overwhelmed at the real size of the world. His perspective shifted, and when Charlie came home he turned his back on the river. He got a job as a timber faller after his discharge, sawing down trees and leaving moonscape behind him. "I went hog wild then," he will explain. "We just took the cream timber. We didn't put nothing back." He became an alcoholic. He made more than one unsuccessful marriage. Then he cracked up his car and spent a few years on crutches, limping from doctor to doctor and going into debt looking for someone to put him back on his feet.

Now Charlie believes that all his bad luck was no more than he deserved. In Yurok and Karuk traditions, crimes aren't forgotten until they're paid for. Charlie says that sickness is one way of paying off debt, and that healing won't come until the last installment is made.

His conversion came when he visited Florence Jones, the Wintu doctor, and she healed him. Charlie came away a convert, an evangelist for the old traditions, a born-again Indian. His duty clear, he ignored the Karuk elders who criticized him and the whites who laughed at him, and jumped into the GO road controversy to protect his praying ground. "You don't want some guy sawing a tree down right there while you're trying to protect his world," he said.

Charlie Thom spoke at rallies, saying things like "Once that GO road goes in, you can kiss this world good-bye." He described the nature of the country the Indians wanted to protect, and didn't leave out the night he almost ran over Bigfoot himself, standing in the road, seven feet tall and hairy as a grizzly. "It was two years before I could even talk about it," Charlie said. He even volunteered to bless the salmon run down the Klamath for the television cameras. The cameras recorded Charlie praying over the gill nets and, when Charlie had finished, a young Yurok man saying, "I never saw anyone do that before."

Nor was Charlie Thom's apprentice afraid of publicity. Charlie was training a young man, Bobby Lake, who claimed that the conditions around the medicine rocks had stopped him from becoming a medicine man. Bobby and his wife, who descends from the most famous doctoring families on the Klamath, prepared for their trial in the high country by abstaining from sex and fasting for ten days. "Then we made that long hike all the way up there only to find out that there's people trying to blow out the side of the mountain," Bobby remembered. "There's trucks hauling out rocks and gravel every few minutes. There's anthropologists and surveyors and curiosity-seekers scampering all over the mountains.

"And then it starts raining down on us, because these people are dirty. They're desecrating this power center. So the Great Creator sends in the sweepers. So here we are. We're stuck way up on this mountainside and we've got to walk forty-eight miles back down in the cold, pouring rain. It's just very discouraging and frustrating."

"How can he go up to the mountains and pray?" Charlie asked. "How can he balance the forces of the world and bring it home to his people with all that destruction going on?"

Despite Charlie's praying and Bobby's speaking, and all the efforts of Sam Jones and other Yuroks, a request made to the court by the Indians jointly with nine environmental organizations for a restraining order to stop construction on the Dillon-Flint section of road was denied. The section was finished in 1976. The court found that the law required the Forest Service merely to hear public opinions regarding its policies, not that it implement them. Only 6.02 miles of road, the Chimney Rock section, was left to pave. Nineteen million dollars had been spent to build the little highway in the mountains. The process of compiling an environmental impact statement for the Chimney Rock section began at Six Rivers, while a series of administrative appeals from lawyers at the Indian Legal Services offices—an agency founded by Sam Jones that used to conduct its business from his dining room—reached successively higher levels of Forest Service administration and were continually denied.

The Forest Service did not consider itself unsympathetic to the position of the few vocal Indian elders. It had commissioned no fewer than a dozen anthropological reports to check the pulse of the Indian religion, and the overwhelming consensus was that the religion was alive and functioning in the high country. On the basis of these studies, several thousand acres of the Siskiyou mountains became eligible for protection as a national historic district. The Forest Service's proposed plan for the final section of the GO road, revealed in the Chimney Rock Environmental Impact Statement released in 1982, routed the road right through the middle of the district. In a public meeting the people who objected to this route were told not to worry. The asphalt was black, and it would blend right in.

By 1983 the Forest Service had a construction crew under contract to complete the road. Ever concerned with the county's unemployment statistics, the Forest Service hired a contractor who promised he would hire the bulk of his thirty-five-man crew from severely depressed Del Norte County.

The county's economic plight had never been worse. A quarter of the county's workers found themselves jobless. Mills were closing, or cutting down their operations, and people were blaming their troubles not on the national slump in timber demand but on the success of the conservationists with the Forest Service and with Congress. "The economics of this area are determined by the fact that most of the land is non-private," said one mill manager. "The availability of timber is essential to the county, and the Forest Service controls the timber."

A map in his office shows the places the loggers can't touch. Roadside views have been removed from timber sales, and streamside watersheds must be left alone. The Smith is protected as a state-designated wild and scenic river. Forty-eight thousand acres had been added to Redwood National Park in 1978 in order to protect the Tall Trees grove from being toppled by erosion upstream on Redwood Creek. Wildernesses have been established in the Trinities, in the Kalmiopsis, in the Marble Mountains, and conservationists have been pushing since the

1960s to protect the Siskiyou crest—an area that includes the GO road and the sacred high country. "All this has been locked up since 1970," the mill manager said. "I think the conservationists have a vendetta against us. If this place is going to be anything but a McDonald's stop on the way to San Francisco, we have got to have timber!"

By 1983, Sam and Lowana were both in their seventies, and they were preparing to defend their Yurok religion against the Forest Service in federal court. The Forest Service had spent a quarter of a million dollars on an anthropological report that reversed earlier studies and found that, without a doubt, Yurok, Karuk, and Tolowa religious practitioners were active in the sacred high country. The study insisted that the GO road and attendant logging would destroy any hope these tribes had for religious regeneration.

Charlie Thom had already lost hope for religious regeneration among his people. By 1983 he had moved to Yreka, near the eastern boundary of the Old Karuk territory, where he lived in a crowded mobile home whose one large window overlooked Mount Shasta. Like Crescent City in Del Norte County, Yreka depends heavily on the lumber industry, and as in Crescent City, mechanization of the mills and sluggish timber sales had put hundreds of people out of work. No one in Yreka, however, was pressuring the Forest Service to finish the GO road: the estimated 203 jobs the Forest Service had predicted would arise in Del Norte with the completion of the road would probably be skimmed from mills in Yreka.

Economic hard times hit the Indian community first, and with more force. Among the troubles that came with it was alcoholism. By 1983, the alcoholism counselor at the Yreka Indian Services Agency was Charlie Thom, plainclothes medicine man. He had left the protection of the high country in what he hoped were the capable hands of Sam Jones and his Yurok supporters and withdrawn from the fight. He had been severely criticized by the Karuk elders for freely informing anyone who asked about his medicine practices, and he had been ignored by the Forest Service. "Trying to talk to the foresters I met, they wouldn't listen or so much as give me a hoot," he wrote to the Forest Service. "Whether they will protect this area or not remains to be seen. They think I am some kind of nut." Charlie says that he moved to Yreka because of a dream that told him the spirit of Mount Shasta was getting restless for lack of attention from its Indians, and that it was his duty to fill the gap. Not long after he moved to Yreka, Mount St. Helens exploded, an eruption that Charlie Thom blames on the lax Indians of Oregon, who should have been watching their mountain.

A coalition was assembled that included Sam and Lowana, another Yurok elder, Jimmie James, who also trained younger people in prayer, and Chris Peters, a Yurok and Karuk man of thirty-three who often brought his own small children to the high country. The Northwest Indian Cemetery Protective Association joined the suit. That association had arisen when an elderly Yurok man named Milton Marks, who lived near the coast at Stone Lagoon, woke up one morning to find a small group of archaeology students digging at the lagoon's perimeter, searching for bones and relics. Marks knew they'd find something if they kept looking—his own aunt and uncle were buried there. Although the plaintiffs included six environmental organizations and two concerned citizens and alleged violations of nearly a dozen laws, Indian religious practices were affected by only two: the First Amendment to the Constitution, guaranteeing freedom of religion; and the American Indian Religious Freedom Act of 1978, which requires federal agencies to consider the protection of Indian religious freedom when evaluating their policies.

Although the latter act had been passed five years before the GO road suit, Indians had yet to win a case with it. When Indians claimed in 1980 that the Tennessee Valley Authority had violated their rights by permanently flooding access to their praying grounds, they lost the case. In 1981, another court had refused to keep tourists from the sacred Rainbow Bridge monument, and in 1982 the Crow tribe of South Dakota had been ordered by the court to yield to road crews when they protested over a road that went right through the Crow ceremonial grounds in a state park. "I would have put sixty dollars down to bet we won the [GO road] case," Sam Jones said, "but the Indian lawyer told me not to waste my money."

* * * * *

The trial was scheduled to take place in San Francisco in May 1983. Sam and Audrey picked up Lowana and they made the eight-hour drive together. They checked into a room in a small motel near downtown San Francisco, with Audrey and Lowana sharing a room.

The trial began badly for the Indian interests. It seemed to Lowana, she later told people, that Judge Stanley Weigel was impatient and angry at the Indian people who had testified, and the young Indian lawyers, inexperienced in federal cases, had also earned his reprimand. At times the testimony of the Indians had appeared contradictory, as if each witness were describing some private dogma to the court. On guard lest the court be trifled with, the judge had been annoyed. Lowana said she wondered if he hadn't already made up his mind to favor the Forest Service.

Lowana always claimed to have been born with a short circuit in her brain, because of which she never felt fear. After the first day of the trail, she says she still wasn't afraid, but she was glad for the urgent consultation with Florence Jones, the Wintu Indian doctor. Florence Jones is a mild, motherly woman with long gray hair that she wears in two braids when she's making medicine. Both Sam and Charlie Thom, whom she has helped, say she can see things and sometimes even tell what you're thinking. Florence Jones told Sam, Lowana, and Audrey that she'd do what she could, and she prayed over the case. According to Lowana, she came to sense that Judge Weigel was a good and fair man, that there was a certain word that would unlock his heart, and that it was up to them to find it.

Lowana was scheduled to testify the next morning, so she had only one night to find the word, and she prayed all night, and she sang her lucky song over and over. She made such a racket that Audrey couldn't get to sleep. Audrey says that around dawn she finally dozed off, and then she remembers wakening suddenly to the sound of morning birds. When she realized she was in a brick motel in the middle of the city where birds had no right to sound so happy, she sat straight up in bed. "Sorry, Audrey," Lowana said. "I guess I just took you with me back to Doctor Rock."

Lowana claimed to have had seven husbands. With her dancing dark eyes and her fluffy white hair, she was still an attractive woman. When she walked into the courtroom, she saw that the judge was coming up behind her. Her grandmother had taught her that the way the Yurok people judge a man's intentions is to walk before the person, then turn suddenly and look him in the face. She dawdled a bit until the judge came near enough, and then swung round to meet his eye. To her surprise, she said, the judge smiled and asked, "Don't I know you from somewhere?" She replied that to her knowledge they were not yet acquainted, and then she asked the judge if he wouldn't like her to explain to him what was going on at his trial.

On the witness stand, she reported her name, her occupation, and her background. "I was raised as a full-blooded Indian baby should be raised and growed up as one," she said. "We always wanted to protect the top of the mountain, because anyone that knows the Klamath, for the first two miles, it's just rock, stray bluffs, and cliffs. So beyond that God left us a strip about ten miles wide where the Karuks can come and gather their grain, their seeds, and things, and once I heard them say, Do you hunt at Doctor Rock? No, ma'am, we do not hunt at Doctor Rock. It's a sacred place. Nothing is killed at Doctor Rock and Chimney Rock. Chimney Rock is a man's place to go and have—to prove that they can stand anything that comes along and be brave, to face the world."

She explained that, unknown to her people, all the land up to way beyond the mountains had been given away. "In that way we lost everything, and now we are standing on the last peak. Doctor Rock. Chimney Rock. My neighbors have lost a lot of their ceremonial grounds due to mismanagement of the people; not because they were cruel, but because they didn't understand."

The judge interrupted. "Not because they were what?" he asked.

"They were not cruel."

"Cruel?"

"Or unkind. They just didn't understand."

"Who was it that didn't understand?"

"The new people that came into the Indian country."

"By the new people, who do you mean?"

"The white people."

"The white people? Well," said the judge, "you are generous in saying they weren't cruel."

"So here I am today," Lowana continued. "I'm looking back. The Tolowa tribe, which was a great nation at one time, their villages was in the town or the city of Crescent City, Smith River, and all through there. They have nothing of their ceremonial grounds, but many of them go to the high country where they have for thousands of years and prayed where they were told to go, Summit Valley.

"The Karuks, they come over the mountains. There is trails there today and we could show it to you, where those trails are. They are secret to everybody else. There are just a few who know where they are, which lead to the high country, Doctor Rock, Chimney Rock, which is a sacred place."

She talked about how the bones of her ancestors have been pulled from their graves to go floating down the Klamath, and she told about the fish and the traditional foods that were no longer fit to eat because of pollution. "Up on through the Klamath River, if you were to go through there, it would make you sick," she said. "I wrote an article on it once I was so proud of it. Now I am heartsick about it. The mountains have all caved in. Some of the most beautiful streams ... we only have concrete left."

The judge interrupted her to ask if she'd allow him to paraphrase. The lawyer had stopped asking questions long before, and Lowana had been making her own decisions about what words to tell the judge. He said that he understood her to mean that because the land had been taken over, and because of the depredations on the surrounding area, the preservation of the high country had become all the more important. He understood her to say that the high country was all that was left.

When she stood to leave, he courteously cautioned her about the step down. "I want to say something to you," he said. "I don't know where the ball is finally going to bounce. I haven't heard all the evidence. But I think you should go knowing that what you've said has been very helpful."

The hearing took another two weeks, and at the end of May the judge reached his decision. The road interfered with the Indians' free exercise of their religion, and the Forest Service had not been able to prove that the national need for timber was great enough to override the Indians' First Amendment rights. He permanently barred the Forest Service from road building and logging within a 17,000-acre zone in the high country. On alleged violations of the American Indian Religious Freedom Act, he vindicated the Forest Service, which, he found, had taken Indian religious practices into account when it planned the road.

Audrey Jones had arranged a picnic supper for the victory celebration at the community hall beside the Klamath, and people brought salmon and venison and bowl after bowl of potato salad. It was a cautious celebration—cautious because the Forest Service had immediately appealed the decision. There was, if anything, too much food, because fewer people joined in than Audrey had planned for. Lowana was asked for her story again and again, and to everyone she explained, "It was the doctoring. The Indian doctoring." She was asked to speak. "After the whites came, they took our religion and they took our pride, and we called ourselves Mexican and we called ourselves Greek. Because we had no world," she said. "Now our day has come again. Now we have a foothold. We can't stop and say we have won. That's because there are greedy eyes. They have destroyed their country wherever they go through. There's streams you can't even drink out of. I'm glad my days are numbered. I won't have to be here to see all the streams die. I don't hold no grudges, though, 'cause we're just here for a day. There's nothing we own, there's just the privilege to share while we're here. I'm so glad that my people have met for thousands of years, and today I am here with you."

Lowana didn't live to celebrate the day that a 153,000-acre area was legislated into the Siskiyou Wilderness by Congress in the fall of 1984. The new wilderness, as Congress drew it, is divided into two segments, one to the north and one to the south of the proposed GO road corridor. The decision of the appellate court was then pending, and Congress felt constrained by the outcome of the court's deliberations. The medicine rocks were not secure until May 24, 1985, when the court denied the Forest Service's appeal and allowed the decision to stop the GO road to stand.

AFTERWORD

The Bedrock Above

WE measure time in ways we can understand. We count heartbeats: seventy-two per minute. We count seasons: four per year. We count years: threescore and ten per lifetime. Mountains tick by their own time. This mountain was carved by glaciers—tick—ten thousand years. To a mountain, the time between glaciers is a heartbeat.

The counting system of the most primitive people is one, two, and many. More than that seems to defeat them. We try to measure mountains by holding them up to our own limited capabilities; what we cannot grasp, we call powerful. Standing close to a mountain, we can't encompass it all: mountains are powerful.

The mountains have a separate biotic pulse. They are more than walls of planetary interior lifted high and iced white. They are glazed with growth; tilted and slippery, they are precarious platforms for life.

The rules that govern are local, and their variations infinite. Lives by the millions mesh on the slopes as tightly as gears. They revolve at speeds to match the season, growing and retreating with the widest extremes of temperature and moisture that the planet can produce. Sometimes one hard winter wipes the teeth from a gear entirely, and it spins suddenly to nothing. But the sharpest teeth, we find, are our own. We have discovered that the catastrophic flooding of the rivers of the Indian plain along the Himalaya, floods that yearly destroy animals, cropland, and human lives, has begun to intensify. We agree that the floods are not acts of God but of human beings. Mining dust fills a high valley, burying a flowered meadow in a deep grave of sludge. Avalanches bulldoze through alpine villages whose surrounding slopes are no longer protected by forests. With our little tools, our intrusions can make a desert of a mountain.

The grand scale confuses us; the mountains, perhaps, block our foresight. They rise, fold and slip, thrust and overthrust through ages. They erode. They are filed smooth by wind and water, their slopes are gentled, and they rise some more. Their rivers chisel valleys, and the valleys fill again with sand, pebbles, rocks, and boulders—mountain parings. What first gives way are those beings whose lifespans most nearly resemble our own: the mosses and forests, the bighorn sheep, the fiercely independent communities of mountaineers. What gives way next is the land itself.

If we could climb to the top, take in the drama through the soles of our feet, we might learn to see a new horizon, a new perspective: that of the mountains. Looking back from the peak we could see the plain, stretching toward Omaha, to the Bay of Bengal, to the foggy Pacific coast, back to the lowlands sloshing with people. Looking forward we could see more mountains, frozen whitecaps in a sea of haze, beckoning with prospects of farther horizons. Can we sit on an out-thrust and hear anything other than our own echoes? Can we scratch a mountain? Which of us, in the final tally, is larger? Which of us is on top?